Reading Street Response to Intervention Kit

Program Overview

The *Reading Street Response to Intervention Kit* provides targeted instruction in core English-Language Arts standards for Grades K to 2 in each of the five critical areas of reading instruction: phonemic awareness, phonics and decoding, fluency, vocabulary, and comprehension. The Kit, designed for small-group or one-on-one instruction, includes lessons on core skills, allowing teachers to focus on the skills children need most and help them make rapid progress to achieve grade-level proficiency. For additional information about the *Reading Street Response to Intervention Kit*, see "How to Use This Kit" in the RTI Implementation Guide.

Phonics Teacher's Guide and Student Worktext

The Teacher's Guide portion includes
- three-tiered, differentiated lessons for 30 phonics and decoding topics
- mini-lessons on specific symbol-sound relationships, spelling patterns, phonograms, letter combinations, and other elements of phonics and decoding
- reinforcement for the strategies and routines used in the core program
- word lists to practice and reinforce each phonics and decoding topic

The Student Worktext portion includes
- additional practice
- word cards and other manipulatives
- School+Home activities on every page

Lesson Features
- **Set the scene** introduces the lesson topic to children.
- **Objectives** identify the instructional objectives for children.
- **Materials** list the Worktext components and additional supporting materials for the lesson, such as the Routine Cards.
- **Direct teaching** is provided through explicit teacher modeling and consistent routines.
- **Mini-lessons** for differentiated instruction.
- **Guided practice** for each mini-lesson consists of ample group practice with multiple response opportunities.
- **Independent practice (On Their Own)** allows children to practice with teacher guidance.
- **If…/then…** provides teachers with specific activities for reinforcing skills.

Table of Contents Phonics and Decoding

Grades **K-2**

Scott Foresman
Phonics and Decoding
Teacher's Guide and Student Worktext

Glenview, Illinois
Boston, Massachusetts
Chandler, Arizona
Upper Saddle River, New Jersey

ISBN-13: 978-0-328-47780-7
ISBN-10: 0-328-47780-X
10 V016 18 17 16 15 14 13

Phonics and Decoding Teacher's Guide

Phonics and Decoding Lesson 1
Common Letter-Sound Correspondences

This lesson demonstrates the instruction you will use for Word Lists 1–26.

Objective:
- Teach all consonant and short vowel sounds.

MATERIALS
- Worktext pp. 2–4
  Word Lists 1–9, p. 2
  Word Lists 10–18, p. 3
  Word Lists 19–26, p. 4
- Routine Card 1

Set the scene Remind children that every word is made of sounds and that sounds are blended quickly together to say a word. Explain that letters are used to spell sounds. Today we are going to learn about the letter that spells the sound /m/.

Routine

1 Teach the Letters Write the letters *Mm*, say the name (*m*), and have children repeat after you several times. Tell children that *m* spells the sound /m/. Point to *M*. The name of this letter is capital (uppercase) *M*. What is the name of this letter? Repeat with lowercase *m*. Explain that *m* is a consonant and a consonant is any letter of the alphabet that is not a vowel. Then model writing the letters *Mm* and have children write them.

2 Connect Sound to Spelling Point to something that begins with *m*, such as a map. What sound do you hear at the beginning of *map*? (/m/)

3 Model and Give Examples Model writing the letter *m* to spell the sound /m/. I'll say a word. Listen to the beginning sound. We'll write the letter *m* if the word begins with /m/. Say *mug*. Do you hear /m/? The first sound in *mug* is /m/. Write the letter *m*. Say /m/ with me. Then say a word that does not begin with /m/, such as *cap*. Do you hear /m/? The word *cap* does not begin with *m*. Then repeat the procedure with a word that has *m* as the final consonant, such as *Pam*.

As students become familiar with short vowels, model blending a word such as *mat*. Now we're going to use sounds and letters we know to read words. Write *m* and say /m/. Add *a* and say /a/. Blend *ma*: /m//a/. Add *t* and say /t/. Run your hand under *mat* as you blend the whole word.

4 Guide Practice As in step 3, continue identifying the beginning sound of words. Use the first five words in the Word List. This time have students identify the beginning sound. If students are able, display the words and have students blend them with you using Routine Card 1.

5 Practice and Review Use the Word List to give children practice writing the letter *m* for the sound /m/. Have them recognize whether the word you say starts or ends with the sound /m/. If students are able, display the words and have students blend them. To review Word Lists 1–9, see Worktext p. 2. To review Word Lists 10–18, see p. 3. To review Word Lists 19–26, see p. 4.

Word Lists 1–9

Begin with the initial list. As students progress, continue with the final and medial lists. To review Word Lists 1–9, see Worktext p. 2.

Word List 1 (*Mm, /m/ m*)

Initial	Final	Medial
men	am	lemon
map	jam	number
mug	hum	bumpy
mop	gum	woman
mats	plum	camel

Word List 2 (*Ss, /s/ s, ss*)

Initial	Final	Medial
sip	gas	also
sun	yes	person
six	us	lesson*
Sam	Russ*	bison
sat	mess*	basket

*Use these words to point out that the /s/ sound can also be spelled *ss.*

Word List 3 (*Tt, /t/ t, tt*)

Initial	Final	Medial
tan	at	better*
ten	let	butter*
top	pit	little*
tip	pat	pretty*
tub	bat	letter*

*Point out that /t/ can also be spelled *tt.*

Word List 4 (*Aa, /a/ a*)

Initial	Medial
am	Sam
an	sat
at	cap
apple	Pam
ant	camp
add	ran

Word List 5 (*Cc, /k/ c, ck*)

Initial	Final	Medial
cat	Mac	pocket*
call	tick*	rocket*
car	rock*	socket*
corn	back*	
cold	sick*	

Point out that /k/ can also be spelled *ck.*

Word List 6 (*Pp, /p/ p*)

Initial	Final	Medial
pot	tap	open
pin	sap	super
pat	cup	upon
pet	lap	paper
pan	jump	sleepy

Word List 7 (*Nn, /n/ n*)

Initial	Final	Medial
nap	run	final
nip	an	banjo
Nat	in	many
not	van	under
net	sun	animal

Word List 8 (*Ii, /i/ i*)

Initial	Medial
it	bit
is	tin
in	pig
if	rip
into	lid

Word List 9 (*Ff, /f/ f, ff*)

Initial	Final	Medial
fit	if	safety
fan	roof	wafer
fun	beef	muffin*
fox	leaf	traffic*
fin	stuff*	waffle*

Point out that /f/ can also be spelled *ff.*

Word Lists 10–18

Begin with the initial list. As students progress, continue with the final and medial lists. To review Word Lists 10–18, see Worktext p. 3.

Word List 10 (*Bb*, /b/ *b*)

Initial	Final	Medial
bat	cab	about
bad	tab	cabin
big	nab	number
ball	fib	robot
bit	rib	habit

Word List 11 (*Gg*, /g/ *g*)

Initial	Final	Medial
gab	dig	ago
got	tug	began
get	bag	dragon
gave	wag	sugar
good	fog	tiger

Word List 12 (*Oo*, /o/ *o*)

Initial	Medial
odd	top
olive	pop
option	sob
ox	bop
otter	mom

Word List 13 (*Dd*, /d/ *d*)

Initial	Final	Medial
did	sad	body
dip	mud	medal
dog	pad	spider
dot	nod	study
duck	rid	under

Word List 14 (*Ll*, /l/ *l*, *ll*)

Initial	Final	Medial
lit	fill*	along
lid	Bill*	color
lot	pal	family
lap	ill*	balloon*
log	doll*	hello*

* Point out that /l/ can also be spelled *ll*.

Word List 15 (*Hh*, /h/ *h*)

Initial	
hug	hot
hip	ham
hid	hop
hat	had
him	hit

Word List 16 (*Ee*, /e/ *e*)

Initial	Medial
egg	met
Ed	bed
enter	set
enjoy	leg
end	pet

Word List 17 (*Rr*, /r/ *r*, *rr*)

Initial	Final	Medial
rob	car	cart
rid	for	carrot*
roll	her	furry*
rap	star	parrot*
rag	better	sorry*

* Point out that /r/ can also be spelled *rr*.

Word List 18 (*Ww*, /w/ *w*)

Initial		Medial
web	wit	always
wed	wet	homework
win	well	awake
will	wag	highway
wig	Wes	away

Word Lists 19–26

Begin with the initial list. As students progress, continue with the final and medial lists. To review Word Lists 19–26, see Worktext p. 4.

Word List 19 (*Jj, /j/ j*)

Initial

jam	jot
jag	jab
jet	Jim
jog	Jill
job	jig

Word List 20 (*Kk, /k/ k*)

Initial	Final	Medial
kit	book	baker
kiss	cook	broken
kid	duck*	taken
Ken	took	worker
Kim	pick*	basket

*Point out that /k/ can also be spelled *ck*.

Word List 21 (*Uu, /u/ u*)

Initial	Medial
up	rub
us	dug
under	gum
until	cut
undo	bug

Word List 22 (*Vv, /v/ v*)

Initial	Final	Medial
vet	Bev	never
van	Liv	seven
Val	Lev	river
Vic		clever
vent		shovel

Word List 23 (*Yy, /y/ y*)

Initial

yell	yard
yum	yarn
yap	yellow
yes	yank
yet	yesterday

Word List 24 (*Zz, /z/ z, zz*)

Initial	Final	Medial
zig	fuzz*	puzzle*
zag	jazz*	fuzzy*
Zak	wiz	drizzle*
zap	fizz*	blizzard*
zip	Liz	fizzle*

*Point out that /z/ can also be spelled *zz*.

Word List 25 (*Qq, /kw/ qu*)

Initial

quit	question
quiet	quick
quiz	quart
queen	quarter
quilt	quack

Word List 26 (*Xx, /ks/ x*)

Final

ox	six
ax	box
pox	wax
Max	fox
Fix	mix

Initial Blends and Three-Letter Blends

Objectives:
- Teach concept of initial consonant blends.
- Introduce *l* and *r* blends.
- Introduce initial *s* blends.
- Introduce three-letter initial blends with *s*.

MATERIALS
- Worktext pp. 5–7
- Routine Card 1
- Letter tiles

Set the scene Explain to children that the mini-lessons below teach the concepts of initial blends. This lesson focuses on initial blends with *l, r,* and *s,* as well as on three-letter initial blends with *s.*

Routine **1. Connect Sound to Spelling** Ask children which sounds they hear at the beginning of the words *like* and *rake.* Repeat the initial sound several times. Help children identify the sounds /l/ and /r/ at the beginning of these words. Today you will learn to read and spell words that combine the /l/ and /r/ sounds with other letter sounds you know.

2. Model and Give Examples Ask children which sounds they hear at the beginning of *plug* and *drag.* Use letter tiles or write the letters *pl* and *dr.* Exaggerate the sounds /p/ and /l/ at the beginning of *plug.* Listen to how the letters *p* and *l* blend together in /p//l/. The letters blend, or go together, when you say the word plug. Have children say /p//l/ several times as you point to *pl.* What are the sounds for this letter combination? Repeat with *dr* and the word *drag.*

3. Model Blending Now we're going to use sounds and letters we know to read words. First we'll say the sounds of the letters, and then we'll read the whole word. Write *pl* and say /p//l/. Add *u* and say /u/. Run your hand under the letters as you blend *plu:* /p//l//u/. Add *g* and say /g/. Then run your hand under *plug* as you blend the whole word. Repeat with *drag.*

Mini-Lesson 1   Initial *l* and *r* Blends

Remind children that...
- Blends contain two or more consecutive consonants, each of which is pronounced and blended with the other.
- Initial means "first" or "beginning."
- Consonants *l* and *r* are often part of initial blends.

Word List

plus	flip	drip	prom
blob	glass	cross	trap
club	slid	bran	

Guide Practice
Repeat the routine with more initial *l* and *r* blends. Introduce the *bl, cl, fl, gl* and *sl* blends by using step 2 of the routine. Then repeat step 3 using the words below. Write each blend and ask for its sounds, and then have children blend the whole word with you. Point out that in each word you hear /l/.

blue	clap	floss	glass	slow

Repeat the process with *cr, br, pr,* and *tr* blends and the words below.

crab	brick	proud	train

If... children have difficulty understanding initial *l* and *r* blends,

then... repeat step 2 of the routine with the blends they are having difficulty with.

On Their Own For more practice, see Worktext p. 5 and the Word List. For each word in the Word List, write it on the board, have children spell it with letter tiles, and have them blend the whole word.

 **Initial _s_ Blends**

Remind children that...

- Blends contain two or more consecutive consonants, each of which is pronounced and blended with the other.
- Initial means "first" or "beginning."
- The letter _s_ is often part of initial blends.

Word List

scab	small
spot	snack
swell	still
skin	

Guide Practice

To practice initial blends with _s_, repeat the routine on the previous page with the blends and words below.

Explain that **sc, sp,** and **sw** are initial consonant blends with _s_. Write each blend and ask for its sound. Then write

out the words _scat, spin,_ and _swim_ from the list below. Circle the first two letters in each word and ask for their sounds. Then ask children to blend the words with you. Tell children that **sk, sm, sn,** and **st,** and **sc** are also initial consonant blends. Repeat the process with the words below.

scat	spin	swim	skip
smack	snap	star	

If... children have difficulty reading the words, **then...** reinforce the Sound-by-Sound Blending Strategy on Routine Card 1 with children.

On Their Own For more practice with initial _s_ blends, use the Word List and Worktext p. 6.

Mini-Lesson 3 **Three-letter Initial _s_ Blends**

Remind children that...

- Blends contain two or more consecutive consonants, each of which is pronounced and blended with the other.
- The letter _s_ is often part of three-letter initial blends.

Word List

scribble	splash
stripe	squirt
spring	

Guide Practice

Practice three-letter initial blends with _s_ by repeating the routine with the blends and words below.

Explain that **scr, str,** and **spr** are initial consonant blends. Write them and ask children for the sound. Then spell out the words _scrub, strike,_ and _sprint._ Circle the first three

letters in each word and sound them out for children. Have children blend the whole word with you. Repeat with **spl** and **squ.**

scrub	strike	sprint	split	squish

If... children have difficulty reading the words, **then...** explain that good readers listen to the sounds of letters in their head as they read. Reinforce the concept by using the Sound-by-Sound Blending Strategy on Routine Card 1 with children.

On Their Own For additional practice with three-letter initial _s_ blends, use the Word List and Worktext p. 7 with children.

Phonics and Decoding Lesson 3
Final Blends

Objectives:

- Teach concept of final consonant blends.
- Introduce final **nd, nt, mp,** and **ft** blends.
- Introduce final **lt, ld,** and **lp** blends.
- Introduce final **sk, sp,** and **st** blends.

MATERIALS

- Worktext pp. 8–10
- Routine Cards 1, 2
- Letter tiles

Set the scene Remind children that certain pairs of consonant sounds frequently appear together at the end of words. Today we will practice saying and reading words that end with two sounds blended together.

Routine **1. Connect Sound to Spelling** Connect today's lesson to previously learned sound-spellings. Write *flap* and *swim.* What do you know about the first sounds in these words? (*Flap* begins with /f//l/ spelled *fl. Swim* begins with /s//w/ spelled *sw.*) Today you'll learn to spell and read words that end in two sounds blended together.

2. Model and Give Examples Ask children which sounds they hear at the end of *land* and *tent.* Use letter tiles or write the letters *nd* and *nt.* Exaggerate the sounds /n/ and /d/ at the end of *land.* Listen to how the letters *n* and *d* blend together when you say the word *land.* Have children say /n//d/ several times as you point to *nd.* What are the sounds for this letter combination? Repeat with *nt* and the word *tent.*

3. Model Blending Now we're going to use sounds and letters we know to read words. First we'll say the sounds of the letters, and then we'll read the whole word. Write *l* and say /l/. Add *a* and say /a/. Run your hand under the letters as you blend *la:* /l//a/. Add *nd* and say /n//d/. Then run your hand under *land* as you blend the whole word. Repeat with *tent.*

Mini-Lesson 1

Final Blends *nd, nt, mp,* and *ft*

Remind children that...

- Blends contain two or more consecutive consonants, each of which is pronounced and blended with the other, as *cl* in *clock.*
- Consonant sounds are sometimes blended together at the end of a word.
- The final blends **nd, nt, mp,** and **ft** are used in many words.

Word List

hand	bent	damp	lift
lend	sent	jump	soft

Guide Practice

Repeat the routine above to practice more final blends. First, review the **nd** and **nt** blends by using the sound-by-sound blending as in step 2 of the routine. Then write each blend and ask for its sounds. Have children blend the whole word with you. Remind them that when two

consonants appear together, the sounds that each letter stands for are usually blended together.

ant	pant	bend	send

Repeat the process with the **mp** and **ft** blends in the words below.

dump	ramp	gift	left

If... children have difficulty understanding these final blends,

then... repeat step 2 of the routine with the blends they are having difficulty with and reinforce with the sound-by-sound blending strategy on Routine Card 1.

On Their Own For additional practice with *nd, nt, mp,* and *ft* final blends, use the Word List and Worktext p. 8. Use letter tiles to spell each word on the Word List. Ask children to point out and say the final blends.

 **Final Blends *lt, ld,* and *lp***

Remind children that...

- Blends contain two or more consecutive consonants, each of which is pronounced and blended with the other.
- Consonant sounds are sometimes blended together at the end of a word.
- The final blends *lt, ld,* and *lp* are used in many words.

Word List

felt	cold	help
melt	wild	scalp

Guide Practice

To practice *lt, ld,* and *lp* blends, repeat the routine on the previous page with the words below. Explain that *lt, ld,* and *lp* are final blends that begin with the consonant *l.* Write each blend. What sounds do you hear? Practice the sound-by-sound blending as in step 2 of the routine. Then write the words below or use letter tiles. Point to the last two letters in each word. Do you hear /l/? Have children practice blending each word.

belt	salt	held	old	gulp	yelp

If... children have difficulty with *lt, ld,* and *lp* blends, **then...** exaggerate the final sounds in each word as you point to the last two letters and have students repeat after you.

On Their Own For more practice with *lt, ld,* and *lp* blends, use Worktext p. 9. For additional practice, use the Word List. Before you say each word, remind children that when *l* and another consonant appear together at the end of a word, the sounds are blended together. Have them practice blending each word with you.

Mini-Lesson 3 **Final Blends *sk, sp,* and *st***

Remind children that...

- Blends contain two or more consecutive consonants, each of which is pronounced and blended with the other.
- Consonant sounds are sometimes blended together at the end of a word.
- The final blends *sk, sp,* and *st* are used in many words.

Word List

ask	crisp	cast
desk	gasp	list

Guide Practice

Practice the *sk, sp,* and *st* blends by repeating the routine with the words below. Explain that *sk, sp,* and *st* are final consonant blends. Write each blend and ask for its sounds. After you repeat each blend, ask children to repeat it. Then write the words below and circle the final two letters of each one. Continue with sound-by-sound blending as in step 3. Have children blend the whole word with you.

mask	risk	grasp	wasp	cost	rest

If... children have difficulty reading the words, **then...** explain that good readers listen to the sounds of letters in their head as they read. Reinforce the concept by using the blending strategy on Routine Card 2 with children.

On Their Own For additional practice with *sk, sp,* and *st* blends, use Worktext p. 10 with children. Provide more practice with the Word List and letter tiles. Write each word and have children spell it with letter tiles. Then have them blend the whole word. Monitor and provide corrective feedback.

Consonant Digraphs

Objectives:

- Teach concept of consonant digraphs.
- Introduce **/sh/ *sh*** digraph.
- Introduce **/th/ *th*** digraph.
- Introduce **/f/ *ph*** and **/f/ *gh*** digraphs.

MATERIALS

- Worktext pp. 11–13
- Routine Cards 1, 2, 8
- Letter tiles

Set the scene Explain that this lesson introduces the concept of consonant digraphs, two consonants that stand for a single sound. The mini-lessons focus on **/sh/ *sh*, /th/ *th*, /f/ *ph*,** and **/f/ *gh*.**

Routine **1. Connect Sound to Spelling.** Write *slip* and *swim.* Remind children that they can read words like these already. What do you know about the first two sounds in these words? (The two consonant sounds are closely blended together.) Practice blending the *sl* and the *sw* sounds with children several times. Today we will learn to read and spell words with two consonants that stand for one sound.

2. Model and Give Examples Write *shark.* Say it aloud several times. The first sound in *shark* is /sh/. Say it with me several times: /sh//sh//sh/. Explain that /sh/ can be spelled *sh.* Have children say /sh/ several times as you point to the letters *sh.* What is the sound of these letters? Write *wish* and follow this procedure with the final /sh/ in *wish.*

3. Model Blending Now we're going to use sounds and letters we know to read words. First we'll say the sounds of the letters, and then we'll read the whole word. Write *sh* and say /sh/. Add *i* and say /i/. Add *p* and say /p/. Run your hand under *ship* as the children blend the whole word with you: /sh//i//p/. Repeat the process several times. Then follow the same procedure to model blending *rush.*

Mini-Lesson 1 — Consonant Digraph /sh/ *sh*

Remind children that...

- Digraphs are two consecutive letters that stand for a single sound, such as *sh* or *th.*
- Some consonant digraphs may appear at the beginning or end of a word.
- The consonant digraph **/sh/ *sh*** is used in many words.

Word List

sheep	dish
shell	fish
shop	push

Guide Practice

Repeat the routine above with the words below to help children connect **/sh/** with **sh.** Write each word. Have children say /sh/ several times as you point to the letters *sh* in each word. The /sh/ can appear at the beginning of some words and at the end of other words. Next, blend each whole word, using step 3 of the routine. Have children blend each word with you several times.

she   show   wash   wish

If... children cannot read a word,
then... have children use sound-by-sound blending for decodable words (Routine Card 1) or have them say and spell high-frequency words (Routine Card 8).

On Their Own For additional practice with the /sh/ *sh* digraph, use Worktext p. 11 and help children read the words on the Word List. Write each letter or digraph and ask for its sound. Run your hand under the word as you blend it several times. Then have children blend the word with you several times. Repeat for each word.

 **Mini-Lesson 2** ## Consonant Digraph /th/ *th*

Remind children that...

- Digraphs are two consecutive letters that stand for a single sound.
- Some consonant digraphs may appear at the beginning or end of a word.
- The consonant digraph **/th/ *th*** is used in many words.

Word List

thank	**bath**
thick	**math**
thin	

Guide Practice

To help children read and spell words with **/th/ *th*,** repeat the routine on the previous page with the words below.

Write *path.* Point to the letters *th.* The letters *th* spell one sound: /th/. Ask children to say /th/ several times. Then blend *path,* using step 3 of the routine. Run your hand

under each word as you blend the sounds: /p//a//th/. Have children blend the word several times with you and then on their own. Repeat the process with the remaining words. Sometimes /th/ appears at the start of a word and other times at the end.

path   that   they   with

If... children have difficulty reading a word,
then... have them use sound-by-sound blending for decodable words (Routine Card 1).

On Their Own For more practice with the /th/ *th* digraph, use Worktext p. 12 and the Word List. Provide children with letter tiles and help them spell *bath.* Say *bath.* Ask children to blend the word with and without you. Repeat with each word.

Mini-Lesson 3 ## Consonant Digraphs /f/ *ph* and /f/ *gh*

Remind children that...

- Digraphs are two consecutive letters that stand for a single sound.
- The letters **ph** and **gh** are used to spell /f/ in many words.

Word List

Phil	**rough**
phoned	**tough**
graph	

Guide Practice

Use sound-by-sound blending (Routine Card 1) and whole-word blending strategies to help children connect **/f/** with **ph** and **gh.** Write *ph.* Explain that the sound /f/ can be spelled *ph.* Have children say /f/ as you point to *ph.* Write *phone.* The letters *ph* spell the sound /f/ as in the word *phone.* Now listen to how I blend this word. Point to each spelling as you say its sound. Then run

your hand under *phone* as you blend the whole word with the children. Repeat with *photo.*

Write *gh.* Explain that the sound /f/ can also be spelled *gh.* Repeat the above process with /f/ *gh* and *cough* and *laugh.* When you see the spelling *ph* or *gh* in a word, try the sound /f/.

phone   photo   cough   laugh

If... children cannot read a word,
then... say /f/ as you point to *ph* or *gh* and blend each whole word (Routine Card 2).

On Their Own For additional practice, see the Word List and Worktext p. 13.

More Consonant Digraphs

Objectives:

- Teach concept of consonant digraphs.
- Introduce **/ch/** *ch* digraph.
- Introduce **/ch/** *tch* digraph.
- Introduce **/hw/** *wh* digraph.

MATERIALS

- Worktext pp. 14–16
- Routine Cards 1, 8
- Letter tiles

Set the scene Remind children that two consonants can spell one sound. Today we will focus on the consonants *ch, tch,* and *wh* and learn how they work together to spell one sound.

Routine **1. Connect Sound to Spelling** Connect today's lesson to previously learned sound-spellings. Write *shin* and *thin.* What do you know about reading these words? (The sound /sh/ is spelled *sh;* /th/ is spelled *th.*) Today you will learn to read and spell words with /ch/ spelled *ch.*

2. Model and Give Examples Write *chalk.* This is *chalk.* The first sound in *chalk* is /ch/. Say it with me: /ch/. Point to *ch.* The sound /ch/ can be spelled *ch.* The letters *c* and *h* work together to spell /ch/. Have children say /ch/ several times as you run your hand under the letters *ch.* What is the sound for these letters?

3. Model Blending Now we're going to use sounds and letters we know to read words. We'll say the sounds of the letters first, and then we'll read the whole word. Write *ch* and say /ch/. Add *i* and say /i/. Add *n* and say /n/. Then run your hand under *chin* as you blend the whole word: /ch//i//n/. Have children say the word with you several times. Follow this procedure to model blending *rich.* Explain that in *chin,* /ch/ appears at the beginning of the word. In *rich,* /ch/ appears at the end of the word.

Mini-Lesson 1 Consonant Digraph /ch/ *ch*

Remind children that...

- Consonant digraphs are two consecutive consonants that stand for a single sound.
- Some digraphs may appear at the beginning or end of a word.
- The consonant digraph **/ch/** *ch* is used in many words.

Word List

chat	beach
chest	much
chill	touch

Guide Practice

To practice the **/ch/** *ch* digraph, repeat the routine above with the words below.

Remind children that the consonants *ch* work together to spell one sound: /ch/. As you write the words, run your hand under the letters *ch* as you say each word. What

sound do these letters spell? Remind children that the /ch/ sound can appear at the beginning of some words and at the end of other words. Have children blend each word with you, using step 3 of the routine. Practice blending each word without pausing between sounds.

check   **chop**   **teach**   **ranch**

If... children have difficulty reading a word,

then... repeat step 2 of the routine with the /ch/ *ch* digraph and have them use sound-by-sound blending for decodable words (Routine Card 1).

On Their Own Use the Word List and Worktext p. 14 for additional practice with the /ch/ *ch* digraph. Tell children that when they see *ch* together in a word, try /ch/.

 **2** **Consonant Digraph /ch/ *tch***

Remind children that…
- Consonant digraphs are two or more consecutive consonants that stand for a single sound.
- The consonant digraph **/ch/ *tch*** is used at the end of many words.

Word List

catch	scratch
match	hitch
pitch	

Guide Practice

Help children practice the **/ch/ *ch*** consonant digraph by using the routine on the previous page. Write the words below. What do you know about reading these words?

Tell children that the letters *tch* stand for one sound: /ch/. Point to the *tch* in each word. The sound /ch/ can be spelled *tch*. When you see these letters together

in a word, try /ch/. Blend each word and then have children blend each word with you without pausing between sounds.

itch   **patch**   **stitch**   **watch**

If… children have difficulty reading words with the /ch/ *tch* consonant digraph,

then… exaggerate /ch/ as you say each word several times. Use the sound-by-sound blending strategy on Routine Card 1.

On Their Own To reinforce the /ch/ *tch* digraph, see Worktext p. 15. Provide additional practice with the Word List and letter tiles. Help children use letter tiles to spell each of the words on the list. Model blending each word as you point to its sounds. Then have children repeat each word with you.

Mini-Lesson 3 **Consonant Digraph /hw/ *wh***

Remind children that…
- Consonant digraphs are usually two consecutive consonants that stand for a single sound.
- The consonant digraph **/hw/ *wh*** is used at the beginning of many words.

Word List

whale	whip
wheel	whisper
where	white

Guide Practice

Use the routine on the previous page to connect **/hw/** with **wh** and to blend words with **wh.**

The sound /hw/ is spelled *wh*. When you see these letters together at the beginning of a word, try /hw/. Then write each word below. Model blending each word as in step 3. Run your hand under each word as you say its sounds

slowly. Ask children to say each word with and without you several times.

what   **when**   **which**   **why**

If… children cannot read a word,

then… say /hw/ aloud as you point to *wh* at the beginning of each word. Also use Routine Card 8 to help children say and spell these high-frequency words.

On Their Own For additional practice with the /hw/ *wh* digraph, use Worktext p. 16 with children. Provide additional practice with the Word List and letter tiles. Help children spell each word with letter tiles. Then have them blend the whole word without pausing between sounds.

Note: In some dialects *wh* is pronounced /w/ rather than /hw/.

Final Digraphs and Sounds

Objectives:
- Teach concept of final digraphs and sounds.
- Introduce final **/j/ *dge.***
- Introduce final **ng, nk.**
- Introduce final **/k/ *ck.***

MATERIALS
- Worktext pp. 17–19
- Routine Cards 1, 2
- Letter tiles

Set the scene Remind children that a sound can be spelled with a letter or a combination of letters. In this lesson, we will learn how to read words that end with the letters *dge, ng, nk,* and *ck.*

Routine **1. Connect Sound to Spelling** Connect today's lesson to previously learned sound-spellings. Write *Jack* and *Jill.* Ask children what they know about the first sound in these words. (It is spelled with the letter *j.*) Have children practice saying /j/ with you several times. Today we will learn to spell and read words with /j/ spelled *dge.*

2. Model and Give Examples Write *jet.* This is *jet.* The first sound in *jet* is /j/. Say it with me. Write the letters *dge* and point to them. The sound /j/ can be spelled *dge.* Have children say /j/ several times as you point to the letters *dge.* What is the sound for these letters?

3. Model Blending Now let's practice reading words. We'll say the sounds of the letters first, and then we'll read the whole word. Write *f* and say /f/. Add *u* and say /u/. Add *dge* and say /j/. Then run your hand under *fudge* as you blend the whole word: /f//u//j/, *fudge.* Have children practice saying *fudge* several times without pausing between sounds. Follow this procedure to model blending *ledge.* Remind children that /j/ can be spelled *dge.* When you see these letters together at the end of a word, try the sound /j/.

Mini-Lesson 1 — Final /j/ *dge*

Remind children that...
- Consonants can work together to spell one sound.
- Final sounds can be spelled with a combination of letters.
- The sound **/j/** spelled ***dge*** is used at the end of many words.

Word List

badge	nudge
fudge	pledge
lodge	

Guide Practice

Help children connect **/j/** to ***dge*** by repeating the previous routine. Ask children to repeat /j/ with you. What sound do the letters *dge* spell?

Write the words below. Now let's practice reading and saying words that end with /j/, spelled *dge.* For each word, point to the initial consonant or blend and say its sound(s). Next, point to the vowel, say its sound, and blend the first two sounds of the word. Then, point to the letters *dge.* Now blend the whole word. Model blending each sound as you point to it and have children blend with and without you.

bridge	**dodge**	**edge**	**judge**

If... children have difficulty reading a word,
then... say /j/ aloud as you point to *dge.* Then return to the word and use Routine Card 2 to help children blend the word.

On Their Own For additional practice reading words that end with *dge,* use Worktext p. 17 and the Word List. Provide children with letter tiles and help them spell and say each word.

Mini-Lesson 2 — Final /ng/ *ng* and /ngk/ *nk*

Remind children that...
- Final sounds can be spelled with a combination of letters.
- The sounds **/ng/** spelled **ng** and **/ngk/** spelled **nk** are used at the end of many words.

Word List

bang	drink
bring	honk
sing	junk

Guide Practice
Use the routine on the previous page to help students connect **/ng/** with **ng** and **/ngk/** with **nk** and to blend words with these sound-spellings.

Write the word *king* and say it aloud. This is the word *king.* The ending sound in *king* is /ng/. Have children repeat /ng/ several times. Point to the letters *ng* as they say /ng/. The sound /ng/ is spelled *ng.* Then practice sound-by-sound blending of *king* as in step 3. Follow the same procedure to introduce /ngk/ spelled *nk,* as in *bank.* Repeat with the remaining words.

king	ring	sang
bank	pink	skunk

If... children cannot read a word,
then... have them use sound-by-sound blending for decodable words (Routine Card 1).

On Their Own For more practice reading words with final sounds /ng/ and /ngk/, see Worktext p. 18. Provide additional practice with the Word List. Tell children to say the sounds in each word to themselves before reading the word aloud. Remember that the letters *ng* spell /ng/ and the letters *nk* spell /ngk/.

Mini-Lesson 3 — Final /k/ *ck*

Remind children that...
- Final sounds can be spelled with a combination of letters.
- The sound **/k/** spelled **ck** is used at the end of many words.

Word List

buck	pack
duck	rock
kick	

Guide Practice
Remind children that sounds can be spelled different ways You learned that the sound /k/ can be spelled with *k,* as in *keep.* Today we will learn to read and spell words with **/k/** spelled **ck.**

Write *ck.* Point to the letters. The sound /k/ can be spelled *ck.* When you see *ck* at the end of a word, try the sound /k/. Have children repeat /k/ with you. Then add the *b* and *a* to form *back.* Model blending as in step 3 of the routine. Run your finger under each sound to say the word: /b//a//k/, *back.* Continue with the other words below. Ask children to say each word with you without pausing between sounds.

back	lock	luck	neck	pick

If... children have difficulty reading words,
then... say /k/ aloud as you point to *ck.* For decodable words, ask children to say each of the sounds.

On Their Own For more practice with the sound /k/ *ck,* use Worktext p. 19 with children. Provide additional practice with the Word List.

Short Vowel Phonograms

Objectives:
- Teach concept of phonograms.
- Introduce short *a* phonograms.
- Introduce short *o* and *i* phonograms.
- Introduce short *u* and *e* phonograms.

MATERIALS
- Worktext pp. 20–22
- Routine Cards 1, 2, 4
- Letter tiles

Set the scene Remind children that words are made up of consonant and vowel sounds. You learned that /a/ is spelled with the letter *a*, and you learned how to blend letters to read words with this sound. Today we will learn another way to read words with the short *a* sound.

Routine **1. Connect** Connect today's lesson to previous learning. Write and say *mat* and *ham.* These are words you know. Let's read them together. Explain that today children will learn a new way to read these words and other words by identifying the word parts *-at* and *-am.* Knowing how to read *-at* and *-am* can help you read many words with these word parts.

2. Model and Give Examples Read *mat* aloud again: *mat.* Have children say *at* with you several times. *Mat* is one of many words with the word part *-at.* Help students think of other words that rhyme with *mat,* such as *cat, hat,* and *flat.* Now write *ham.* Repeat the process to introduce children to words with the word part *-am,* such as *jam, slam,* and *ram. Ham* is one of many words with the word part *-am.*

3. Model Blending Write *at* and slowly blend it several times with children. Then write *m* at the beginning. Cover the word part *-at* and point to *m.* Say *m* aloud: /m/. Then cover *m* and read the word part *-at* aloud: *at.* When you see a word with *-at* at the end, notice the two parts in the word. Look at the word part that comes before the vowel and read the parts one after the other. The two parts are *m* and *-at.* Let's read together: *m, at, mat.* Erase *m* and write *c,* and blend the word with children. Repeat with *hat* and *flat.* Repeat the procedure with the word part *-am* and the words *ham, jam,* and *Sam.*

Mini-Lesson 1 — Short *a* Phonograms

Remind children that...
- A phonogram is part of a word made up of a vowel and all the letters that follow it, as *-at* in *bat, fat, flat.*
- Many words include short *a* phonograms, such as *-ag, -ap, -ack,* and *-ank.*

Word List
flag	tap	crack	blank
wag	trap	sack	drank

Guide Practice
Remind children that one way to read words is to break them into word parts and read the parts one after the other. Today we're going to identify and read words with different short *a* sounds.

Write *bag.* Have children read the word with you. *Bag* is one of many words with the word part *-ag.* Cover the *-ag* and point to the *b.* What sound does *b* stand for? Say it with me: /b/. Now cover the *b* and read the word part *-ag* aloud. Have children say /ag/ with you. Erase *b* and write *t* to form the word *tag* and repeat the process.

Then repeat this procedure to help children read the words below that end with other short *a* phonograms: *-ap, -ack,* and *-ank.*

bag, tag   map, lap   back, pack   sank, tank

If... children cannot read a word,
then... help them use the word parts strategy (Routine Card 4).

On Their Own To practice short *a* phonograms, use Worktext p. 20 and help children say and read the words on the Word List.

Mini-Lesson 2 — Short *o* and *i* Phonograms

Remind children that...

- A phonogram is part of a word made up of a vowel and all the letters that follow it, as *-ack* in *back, crack, track.*
- Many words include short *o* phonograms, such as *-ot, -op, -ock,* and *-ob.*
- Many words include short *i* phonograms, such as *-ill, -ip, -ick,* and *-ing.*

Word List

dot, spot	dock, clock	will, spill	stick, kick
mop, chop	sob, job	drip, skip	thing, ring

Guide Practice

Repeat step 2 of the routine on the previous page to introduce short *o* and short *i* phonograms. First, introduce the *-ot, -op, -ock,* and *-ob* word parts. Repeat each word part together several times. What do you know about reading words with *-ot, -op, -ock,* and *-ob?* When you see a word with one of these word parts, look at the word part that comes before it. Repeat step 3 of the routine on the previous page, using the words below.

pot, not, rot	**hop, drop, cop**
lock, rock, sock	**job, mob, rob**

Repeat the process with these common short *i* phonograms: *-ill, -ip, -ick,* and *-ing.*

hill, bill, fill	**skip, tip, rip**
pick, sick, lick	**sing, wing, king**

If... children have difficulty reading words with particular phonograms,

then... model blending the word parts one after the other without pausing between sounds, using Routine Cards 1, 2 and 4.

On Their Own For additional practice, see Worktext p. 21 and the Word List. Provide children with letter tiles and help them spell and read the word parts in each word.

Mini-Lesson 3 — Short *u* and *e* Phonograms

Remind students that...

- A phonogram is part of a word made up of a vowel and all the letters that follow it, as *-ill* in *pill, will,* and *spill.*
- Many words include short *u* phonograms, such as *-unk, -ug,* and *-um.*
- Many words include short *e* phonograms, such as *-ell, -ed,* and *-est.*

Word List

sunk, trunk	plum, yum	red, sled
hug, jug	tell, well	rest, chest

Guide Practice

Use step 2 of the routine to help children read words with short *u* and short *e* phonograms. First introduce the *-unk, -ug,* and *-um* word parts and have children repeat each word part with you. Then build each of the word parts with letter tiles. Use the words below to model building new words by adding different letters at the beginning of each word part. Have children say each word with you without pausing between sounds. Look for words with these word parts as you read.

dunk, chunk, bunk	**rug, bug, tug**	**hum, drum, gum**

Repeat the process with these short *e* phonograms: *-ell, -ed,* and *-est.*

fell, bell, spell	**bed, fed, sled**	**best, west, nest**

If... children have difficulty reading word parts,

then... have them identify and say one part at a time as you cover the remaining parts.

On Their Own For additional practice, see Worktext p. 22 and the Word List. Help children build each word with letter tiles. Have them identify the word parts and then read each word as you run your hand beneath the parts.

More Consonant Sounds

Objectives:
- Teach concept of consonant sounds.
- Introduce soft **/s/ c** sound.
- Introduce soft **/j/ g** sound.
- Introduce **/z/ s** sound.

MATERIALS
- Worktext pp. 23–25
- Routine Cards 1, 2, 4
- Letter tiles

Set the scene Remind children that some sounds can be spelled in more than one way. This lesson focuses on new spellings for the sounds /s/, /j/, and /z/.

Routine **1. Connect Sound to Spelling** Connect today's lesson to previously learned sound-spellings. Write *sock* and *same*. What do you know about reading these words? (Both begin with /s/ spelled *s*.) Repeat /s/ with me: /s//s//s/. Explain that children have been listening to words with /s/. Today you will learn how to spell and read words with /s/ spelled *c*.

2. Model and Give Examples Write *pace*. This is *cent*. The first sound in *cent* is /s/. Say it with me: /s/. Point to the *ce*. When *c* is followed by *e*, *c* usually stands for /s/. Have children say /s/ several times as you run your hand under the letters *ce*. Explain that *c* followed by *i* stands for /s/. Write *city* and repeat the process with *ci*.

3. Model Blending Point to *cent*. This word has the letter *c* followed by an *e* (point to the letters). When *c* is followed by *e* or *i*, it usually spells the sound /s/. This is how I blend this word. Point to each spelling as you say its sound several times. Then run your hand under *cent* as you blend the whole word: /s//e//n//t/ *cent*. Say the sounds quickly to say the word. What's the word? Yes, it's *cent*. Have children blend with you. Follow this procedure to model *city*.

Mini-Lesson 1 — Soft Consonant Sound /s/ c

Remind children that...
- Some sounds can be spelled in more than one way.
- *C* followed by *e* or *i* usually stands for /s/.

Word List

recess	circle
cell	excite
center	pencil

Guide Practice
Use the routine on the previous page with the words below to help children connect **/s/** with **c** and to blend soft **c** words.

When the letter *c* is followed by an *e* or an *i*, it spells the sound /s/. Help children use letter tiles to spell *cell*. What do you notice about the first sound in this word? (The word begins with the sound /s/ spelled with *c* followed by *e*.) Point to *c* and have children say /s/. Now let's blend

this word together: /c//e//l/. Follow step 3 of the routine as you have children say the word with you several times. Run your hand under each letter as children say the word without pausing between sounds. Repeat the procedure with the words below.

cent   celery   cider   circus

If... children have difficulty reading a word,
then... model segmenting the word. Have children blend the word with you (Routine Card 2).

On Their Own Use the Word List and Worktext p. 23 to help children blend more soft *c* words.

 **Mini-Lesson 2** **Soft Consonant Sound /j/ g**

Remind children that...
- Some sounds can be spelled in more than one way, such as /s/, which can be spelled *s* or *c*.
- The sound **/j/ g** (spelled *j* or *g*) is used in many words.

Word List

gem	giant
germ	ginger
giraffe	gerbil

Guide Practice

Help children understand that the sound **/j/** can be spelled **g** by using the routine on the previous page with the words below.

Write *jet* and *June.* What do you know about the first sound in these words? (Both words begin with /j/ spelled *j.* Today you'll learn to spell and read words with /j/ spelled *g* followed by *e* or *i.* Now write *gem.* Point to

the letters *ge.* When *g* is followed by *e,* it often spells the sound /j/. Run your hand under *gem* as you blend the whole word: /j//e//m/. Have children blend *gem* with you. Repeat the procedure with the words below.

gentle   genius   gigantic   region

If... children have difficulty with the /j/ *g* sound, **then...** exaggerate /j/ as you say each word. Use the sound-by-sound blending strategy on Routine Card 1.

On Their Own To reinforce the /j/ *g* sound, see Worktext p. 24. Provide additional practice with the Word List and letter tiles. Remind children to try /j/ when they see words with *ge* or *gi.*

Mini-Lesson 3 **Consonant Sound /z/ s**

Remind children that...
- Some sounds can be spelled in more than one way, such as /j/ (*j* or *g*).
- The sound **/z/ s** is used in many words.

Word List

as	his
bells	rose
dogs	use

Guide Practice

Remind children that some consonant sounds can be spelled in more than one way. Today we will learn about the sound **/z/** spelled **s.** Use the routine on the previous page to read and say words with this sound-spelling.

Write *zip* and say it aloud. Did you hear /z/? Say it with me: *zip.* The /z/ in *zip* is spelled *z.* One at a time, write each word below. Run your hand under each word as you

model blending sounds. Then have children blend the whole word, as in step 3. Remember that *s* can spell the sound /z/.

has   is   nose   these   those

If... children cannot read the words,
then... say /z/ aloud as you point to *s* in each word. Use Routine Card 4 to help children say and spell high-frequency plural words with *s.*

On Their Own For additional practice with /z/ *s,* use Worktext p. 25. Provide more practice with the Word List and letter tiles. Remind children to say the sounds quickly to say the word.

Phonics and Decoding Lesson 9
Long Vowels

Objectives:
- Teach concept of long vowel sounds.
- Introduce long *a* spelled *a_e.*
- Introduce long *i* spelled *i_e.*
- Introduce long *o* spelled *o_e.*

MATERIALS
- Worktext pp. 26–28
- Routine Cards 1, 2, 7, 8
- Letter tiles

Set the scene Remind children that vowels can have different sounds. You have learned how to read words with short vowel sounds, such as /a/ and /e/. Today we will learn how to read words with the long *a, i,* and *o* sounds.

Routine **1. Connect Sound to Spelling** To connect today's lesson to previously learned sound-spellings, write *cap* and *ran.* You can read words like these. They both have short *a,* /a/, spelled *a.* Repeat the short *a* sound with me: /a//a//a/. Explain that today children will learn how to spell and read words with long *a,* /ā/, spelled *a_e.*
2. Model and Give Examples Write *a_e.* The long *a* sound, /ā/, can be spelled *a_e.* Point to *a_e.* Have children say /ā/ several times as you point to *a_e.* The letter *e* gives the vowel *a* its long sound, and the blank shows where a consonant will go.
3. Model Blending Write *a_e* and say its sound: /ā/. Write *c* and blend the sounds /k/ā/. Have children blend with you as you run your hand under the letters. Write *m* in the blank and have children say its sound with you: /m/. Then blend the whole word, pointing to *a* and *e* as you say /ā/. This is how I blend this word: /k/ā/m/, *came.* Have children practice saying the word without pausing between sounds. Say the sounds quickly to say the word. What's the word? Yes, it's *came.* Follow this procedure to model *made* and *date.* Begin each word by writing the vowel spelling *a_e* as a unit.

Mini-Lesson 1 — Long *a* (spelled *a_e*)

Remind children that...
- Vowels can have different sounds.
- A long vowel sound is a vowel sound that is the same as the name of a vowel letter—*a, e, i, o,* and *u.*
- Many words contain the long **a** sound, /ā/ spelled *a_e.*

Word List
ate	plate
make	skate
name	take

Guide Practice
Use the routine above to help children connect /ā/ with *a_e* and to blend words with the long **a** spelling pattern.

Use letter tiles or write the words below. Say each one aloud several times. What do you know about reading these words? When you see the spelling *a_e* in a word, try the long *a* sound, /ā/. Say /ā/ aloud with children as you point to *a_e.* Model blending the first word, *cake,* using step 3 of the routine. Point to the initial consonant, say its sound, and blend the first two sounds: /k/ā/. Point to the next consonant and say its sound: /k/. Now blend the word with me: /k/ā/k/. Repeat it several times and then move to the next word.

cake   game   tape   safe

If... children have difficulty reading a word,
then... use Routine Cards 1 and 2 to model blending as you point to each sound-spelling.

On Their Own Use the Word List and Worktext p. 26 to help children read more words with /ā/.

Mini-Lesson 2 — Long *i* (spelled *i_e*)

Remind children that...
- Vowels can have different sounds.
- A long vowel sound is a vowel sound that is the same as the name of a vowel letter—*a, e, i, o,* and *u.*
- Many words contain the long *i* sound, /ī/ spelled *i_e.*

Word List
bite	ride
life	side
nice	size

Guide Practice
Use the routine to connect /ī/ with *i_e* and to help children blend words with the long *i* spelling pattern.

Write the words below. When you see the spelling *i_e* in a word, try the long *i* sound. Have children say /ī/ several times as you point to *i_e* in each word. The letter *e* gives the vowel *i* its long sound, and the blank shows where a consonant will go. Run your hand the first word, *bike.* This is how I blend this word: /b//ī//k/. Say it with me several times. Follow this procedure to model the other words.

bike   dive   like   time

If... children have difficulty with the long *i* sound spelled *i_e,*

then... exaggerate /ī/ as you say each word. Use Routine Card 8 for high-frequency words.

On Their Own See Worktext p. 27 and the Word List for additional practice. Help children spell each word with letter tiles. Then have them blend the whole word with and without you.

Mini-Lesson 3 — Long *o* (spelled *o_e*)

Remind children that...
- Vowels can have different sounds.
- A long vowel sound is a vowel sound that is the same as the name of a vowel letter—*a, e, i, o,* and *u.*
- Many words contain the long *o* sound, /ō/ spelled *o_e.*

Word List
bone	smoke
hope	spoke
note	

Guide Practice
Tell children that today they will learn about the long *o* sound and read and say words spelled *o_e.* Write *o_e* and have children say its sound: /ō/.

Write *h* and blend the sounds /h//ō/. Write *m* in the blank and say its sound. Then blend the whole word, pointing to *o* and *e* as you say /ō/. This is how I blend this word: /h//ō//m/, *home.* Let's say it together several times. Repeat the process in step 3 with the other words. Write the vowel spelling *o_e* as a unit first. Remind children that when they see the *o_e* spelling pattern, they should try the long *o* sound.

home   joke   nose   stone   vote

If... children have difficulty reading the words,

then... model breaking each word into sounds. Help children say each sound and write its spelling (Routine Card 7).

On Their Own For additional practice with this long *o* spelling pattern, use Worktext p. 28 and the Word List. Help children blend the sounds of each word with you.

Phonics and Decoding Lesson 10
Other Long Vowel Patterns

Objectives:
- Teach concept of long vowel sounds.
- Introduce long *u* spelled *u_e* and long *e* spelled *u_e*.
- Introduce long *e, o, i* spelled *e, o, i*.
- Introduce long *i* and long *e* spelled *y*.

MATERIALS
- Worktext pp. 29–31
- Routine Cards 1, 3, 8
- Letter tiles

Set the scene Remind children that vowel sounds can be short or long. You have learned how to read words with long vowels *a, i,* and *o,* all spelled with a vowel-consonant-vowel pattern. Today we will learn to read words with these and other long vowel sounds spelled in different ways.

Routine **1. Connect Sound to Spelling** Write *cave, fine,* and *rode.* What do you know about the vowel sounds in these words? (The vowels are long.) Tell children that they will learn to spell and read words with long *u,* /ū/, spelled *u_e* and long *e,* /ē/, spelled *e_e.*

2. Model and Give Examples Explain again that the long *u* sound, /ū/, can be spelled *u_e.* Write *u_e* and have children say /ū/ as you point to the letters. The letter *e* gives the vowel *u* its long sound, and the blank shows where a consonant will go. Repeat the procedure to introduce /ē/ spelled *e_e.*

3. Model Blending Now let's practice reading words with these letter patterns. Write *u_e* and say its sound: /ū/. Write *c* and blend the sounds: /k/ū/. Have children blend with you as you point to the letters. Write *t* in the blank and have children say its sound with you: /t/. Then blend the whole word, pointing to *u* and *e* as you say /ū/. This is how I blend this word: /k/ū/t/, *cute.* Have children practice saying the word without pausing between sounds. Follow this procedure to model the long *e,* /ē/, spelled *e_e* as in *Pete.*

Mini-Lesson 1 — Long *u* (spelled *u_e*) and Long *e* (spelled *e_e*)

Remind children that…
- Vowel sounds can be short or long.
- A long vowel sound is a vowel sound that is the same as the name of a vowel letter—*a, e, i, o,* and *u.*
- Many words contain the long *u* sound, spelled *u_e,* and the long *e* sound, spelled *e_e.*

Word List

cube	complete
mule	Steve
fume	

Guide Practice
Explain that today children will practice reading words with the long *u* sound, /ū/, and the long e sound, /ē/. Use the routine above to introduce children to the vowel-consonant-vowel patterns below.

Write the first two words and say each aloud several times. What do you know about reading *huge* and *use?* When you see the spelling *u_e* in a word, try the long *u* sound, /ū/. Say /ū/ aloud with children as you point to *u_e.* Then point to the initial consonant, say its sound, and blend the first two sounds: /h//ū/. Point to the next consonant and say its sound: /j/. Now blend the word with me: /h//ū//j/. Repeat the procedure with *use* and then introduce /ē/ spelled *e_e.*

huge   use   Eve   Zeke

If… children have difficulty reading a word, **then…** use Routine Cards 1 and 3 to practice sound-by-sound or vowel-first blending.

On Their Own Use the Word List and Worktext p. 29 to help children read more words with /ū/ and /ē/. Provide children with letter tiles.

 **Mini-Lesson 2** **Long *e* (spelled *e*), Long *o* (spelled *o*), and Long *i* (spelled *i*)**

Remind children that...
- A long vowel sound is a vowel sound that is the same as the name of a vowel letter—*a, e, i, o,* and *u.*
- Many words use *e* to spell /ē/, *o* to spell /ō/, or *i* to spell /ī/.

Word List

be	told
she	find
most	so

Guide Practice
Remind children that they learned that /ē/, /ō/, and /ī/ can be spelled with the letters *e, o,* or *i* followed by a consonant and then a silent *e.* Today we're going to learn other ways to spell the sounds /ē/, /ō/, and /ī/.

Write *e.* Have children say /ē/ several times with you. Write *m.* Then blend the whole word: /m//ē/, *me.* When a word or a syllable ends with one vowel, the vowel sound is usually long. Follow this procedure to model the sound /ō/ spelled o and the sound /ī/ spelled *i* to help children read and say the words below.

me	go	cold	no	hi

If... children cannot read a word,
then... have them use sound-by-sound blending (Routine Card 1) or have them say and spell high-frequency words with you (Routine Card 8).

On Their Own See Worktext p. 30 and the Word List for additional practice. Help children spell each word with letter tiles. Have them blend the sounds quickly to say each word.

Mini-Lesson 3 **Long *i* and Long *e* (spelled *y*)**

Remind children that...
- Vowel sounds can be short or long.
- A long vowel sound is a vowel sound that is the same as the name of a vowel letter—*a, e, i, o,* and *u.*
- Many words end with the sounds /ī/ and /ē/ spelled with **y.**

Word List

sky	funny	silly
why	lady	

Guide Practice
Explain to children that vowel sounds can be spelled in different ways. Today we're going to learn that the sounds /ī/ and /ē/ can be spelled with a **y** at the end of a word.

Write *y.* Explain that the long *i* sound can be spelled *y.* Have children repeat /ī/ as you point to *y.* When the letter *y* comes at the end of a one-syllable word, it usually stands for /ī/. Write *by* and have children say it with you. Then write *lucky.* When the letter *y* comes at the end of a word with more than one syllable, it usually stands for /ē/. Have children say *lucky.* Use this procedure to help children read the words below.

fly	try	baby	happy

If... children have difficulty reading the words,
then... explain that when they see the letter *y* at the end of a one-syllable word, try /ī/. If the word has more than one syllable, try /ē/.

On Their Own For additional practice with this sound-spelling, use Worktext p. 31 and the Word List.

Phonics and Decoding Lesson 11
Endings

Objectives:
- Teach concept of inflected endings.
- Introduce endings *-s, -es.*
- Introduce ending *-ed.*
- Introduce ending *-ing.*

MATERIALS
- Worktext pp. 32–34
- Routine Cards 1, 4
- Letter tiles

Set the scene Remind children that many words are made up of smaller word parts. In this lesson, we will learn to add endings to words to make new words. We will learn to read words with the word parts *-s, -es, -ed,* and *-ing.*

Routine **1. Connect** Connect today's lesson to previous learning. Write *book* and *girl.* These are words you know. Let's read them. Today we will learn how to make new words by adding *-s* to these words and other words you know.

2. Model and Give Examples Point to and say *book.* We can add *s* to the end of *book* to make a new word. Add *s.* Cover the word part *-s* and read the base word aloud: *book.* Then cover the base word and read the word part *-s* aloud: /s/. The *-s* in *books* spells the sound /s/. Finally, say the new word: *books. Books* means "more than one book."

3. Model Blending When I see a word with *-s* at the end, I notice the two parts of the word. Let's read the parts one after the other to say the word. Point to *books.* In this word the parts are *book* and *-s.* I read *book, s, books.* Now point to *girl* and add *-s.* Run your hand under *girl.* The first part is *girl.* The second part is *-s.* The *-s* in *girls* spells the sound /z/. Say *girl, s, girls.* Remind them that the sound /s/ at the end of *books* and the sound /z/ at the end of *girls* are both spelled with the letter *s.* Have children read both words with you several times. When we add *-s* or *-es* to some words, we make the words mean "more than one." When we add *-ed* or *-ing* to action words, like *run* and *shout,* we tell when those actions happen.

Mini-Lesson 1 — Ending *-s, -es*

Remind children that...
- Many words are made up of smaller word parts.
- Many words end with the word part *-s* and *-es.*

Word List

adds	tells
cuts	foxes
hums	tosses

Guide Practice
Use step 3 of the routine above to help children read the words below with the word part *-s.* Write *licks.* This word has two parts: *lick* and *-s.* Run your hand under *licks* as you model blending each sound: /l//i//k//s/. The sound /s/ at the end of *licks* and the sound /z/ at the end of *legs* are spelled with the letter *s.*

licks   quits   legs   yells

Repeat this procedure with words that end with *s* or *x* and the word part *-es.*

misses   passes   fixes   mixes

If... children have difficulty reading the words,
then... help children identify the word parts. Read the word with them as you run your hand beneath the parts (Routine Card 4).

On Their Own For additional practice, use the Word List and Worktext p. 32. Help children use letter tiles to spell the base word. Have children add *-s* or *-es* and read the new words aloud.

 **Ending -ed**

Remind children that...

- Many words are made up of smaller word parts, such as -s.
- Many words end with the word part **-ed.**

Word List

fixed	**killed**
tossed	**spelled**
buzzed	

Guide Practice

Today we will learn to make new words by adding the word part **-ed** to words you know. Write *pack* and say it aloud. We can add *-ed* to pack to make a new word. Add *-ed.* Run your hand under the two parts of the word as you say them: *pack, -ed.* Say the word with me: /p//a//k//t/. The *-ed* in *packed* spells the sound /t/.

Now write *filled* and say it aloud. This word has two parts: *fill, -ed.* Say the word with me: *fill, -ed, filled.* The *-ed* in *filled* spells the sound /d/. Have children say the word with you: /f//i//l//d/. Write the remaining words below and repeat the procedure with each of them.

packed   **picked**   **missed**   **filled**   **yelled**

If... children cannot read the words,
then... have them identify one part at a time as you cover the remaining part.

On Their Own See Worktext p. 33 and the Word List for additional practice. Help children use each word in a sentence.

Ending -ing

Remind children that...

- Many words are made up of smaller word parts, such as -s and -ed.
- Many words end with the word part **-ing.**

Word List

adding	**missing**
buzzing	**selling**
fixing	

Guide Practice

Today we will learn about adding the word part **-ing** to words you already know. Write *kick* and read it aloud. We can add *-ing* to the end of *kick* to make a new word. Add *-ing.* Cover the word part *-ing* and read the base word aloud: *kick.* Then cover the base word and read the word part *–ing* aloud: /i//ng/. Finally, say the new word together several times: *kick, -ing, kicking.* When you see a word with *-ing* at the end, remember to read the two

parts, one after the other. Repeat the procedure with the other words below.

kicking   **packing**   **mixing**
telling   **tossing**

If... children have difficulty reading a word,
then... help them blend the individual sounds of the first word part before they read the second word part, *-ing.* Then read the whole word (Routine Cards 1, 4).

On Their Own For additional practice with the ending *-ing,* use Worktext p. 34 and the Word List. Have children read each word and spell it with letter tiles.

Phonics and Decoding Lesson 12
Syllable Patterns

Objectives:
- Teach concept of syllable patterns.
- Introduce syllable pattern **VC/CV**.
- Introduce syllable pattern **V/CV**.
- Introduce syllable pattern **VC/V**.

MATERIALS
- Worktext pp. 35–37
- Routine Cards 1, 4
- Letter tiles

Set the scene Remind children that many words can be broken up into smaller word parts. Today we will learn how to use this strategy with syllables.

Routine **1. Connect** Connect today's lesson to previous learning. Write and read familiar words, such as *passes* and *mixing.* These words have two syllables. The syllables are broken between the base word and the ending. Today we will learn how to read other words that have two syllables.

2. Model and Give Examples Write *napkin.* Have children say the word with you several times: *napkin. Napkin* has two syllables. Circle the *p* and the *k* in the middle of napkin. The word can be divided between the two consonants to break the word into two smaller parts. Point to the first syllable and say it aloud: *nap.* Point to the second syllable and say it aloud: *kin.* Finally say the word: *napkin.* How many syllables does *napkin* have? Yes, it has two syllables.

3. Model Blending Write *contest.* When I see a word with two consonants in the middle, I divide the word after the first consonant. Cover *test.* Say the first syllable with me: *con.* Then cover *con* and read the final syllable aloud: *test.* Now read the syllables one after the other to say the word. The syllables are *con* and *test.* I read: *con, test, contest.* Repeat the process with *mitten.* Point to the *p* and the *k* in *napkin* and the *t* and the *t* in *mitten.* The two consonants in the middle of a word may be the same, or they may be different letters.

Mini-Lesson 1 — Syllable Pattern VC/CV

Remind children that...
- Some words can be broken into smaller word parts.
- A syllable is a word part that contains a single vowel sound.
- Many words contain the syllable pattern **VC/CV**.

Word List
basket	rabbit
hidden	sister
picture	under

Guide Practice
Use step 3 of the routine above to help children read words with the syllable pattern **VC/CV**.

Write *kitten.* When you see a word with two consonants in the middle, divide the consonants after the first one to break the word into two smaller parts. How many parts does *kitten* have? Yes, *kitten* has two parts, or syllables.

What are they? (The first is *kit.* The second is *ten.*) Point to the two syllables. Have children read the syllables one after the other to read the word with you: *kit, ten, kitten.* Repeat this procedure with the remaining words below.

kitten   happen   person   picnic

If... children have difficulty reading word parts, **then...** use Routine Card 4 to help them identify one part at a time as you cover the remaining part.

On Their Own For additional practice, use the Word List and Worktext p. 35. Help children use letter tiles to spell the word. Then have children break each word into two syllables and blend it several times aloud.

Mini-Lesson 2 — Syllable Pattern V/CV

Remind children that…
- Some words can be broken up into smaller word parts.
- A syllable is a word part that contains a single vowel sound.
- Many words contain the syllable pattern **V/CV.**

Word List
table	motel
bonus	music
frozen	pretend

Guide Practice
Use Routine Card 4 to help children read words with the syllable pattern **VC/V.** In today's lesson we will learn to divide words that have only one consonant between vowels.

Write *motor.* Read it aloud: *motor. Motor* has two syllables. We can divide this word into two parts. To divide a word that has a consonant between two vowels, the consonant (point to the *t*) usually goes with the second syllable. That makes the first vowel (point to the *o*) long. Cover *tor* and read the first syllable aloud: *mo.* Then, cover *mo* and read the second syllable aloud: *tor.* Model reading the syllables one after the other. Have children read with you: *mo, tor: motor.* Repeat the procedure with the remaining words.

motor   **polar**   **open**   **student**

If… children cannot read a word,

then… help them identify its two syllables. Read one after the other to say the word.

On Their Own See Worktext p. 36 and the Word List for additional practice. Remind children that the first vowel has a long sound.

Mini-Lesson 3 — Syllable Pattern VC/V

Remind children that…
- Some words can be broken up into smaller word parts.
- A syllable is a word part that contains a single vowel sound.
- Many words contain the syllable pattern **VC/V.**

Word List
camel	model
clever	punish
dragon	seven

Guide Practice
Connect to previous learning to help children read words with the syllable pattern **VC/V.** With some words that have a consonant between two vowels, you divide the word after the first vowel. Write *even.* Identify the two syllables. Say *even.* With other words that have a consonant between two vowels, you need to divide the word in another way.

Write *finish.* If I divide *finish* after the first vowel, the *i* will have a long sound, /ī/. Cover *nish* and say /f//ī/. Uncover *nish* and say the whole word: /f//ī//n//i//sh/. That doesn't sound right. But if I divide the word after the *n*, it makes the vowel in the first syllable short. Say /f//i//n/. Have children say the word with you: *fin, ish, finish.* That sounds right. Repeat with the words below.

finish   **lemon**   **never**   **river**   **visit**

If… children have difficulty reading a word,

then… point out the short vowel sound and blend the word together (Routine Card 1).

On Their Own For additional practice, use Worktext p. 37 and the Word List.

R-Controlled Vowels

Objectives:

- Teach concept of r-controlled vowels.
- Introduce **/är/** *ar.*
- Introduce **/ôr/** *or, ore, oar.*
- Introduce **/èr/** *er, ir, ur.*

MATERIALS

- Worktext pp. 38–40
- Routine Cards 1, 2, 7
- Letter tiles

Set the scene Remind children that letters sometimes join together to spell a new sound. You learned the sounds /a/ spelled *a* and /r/ spelled *r.* Today we will learn about the sounds of vowels when they are followed by **r.**

Routine

1. Connect Connect today's lesson to previously learned sound-spellings. Write *cap.* Ask children what they know about the vowel sound in this word? (It has the short *a* sound, /a/, spelled *a.*) Say *car.* Today you'll learn to spell and read words with *ar.*

2. Model and Give Examples Write *ar.* The sound /är/ is spelled *ar.* Have children say /är/ several times as you point to *ar.* Together, the letters *ar* spell the sound /är/.

3. Model Blending Write *car.* This word has the letters *ar* (point to them), which spell the sound /är/. This is how I blend this word. Point to each spelling as you say its sound: /k//är/. Then run your hand under *car* as you blend the whole word /k/ /är/ several times. Follow this procedure to model *jar* and *star.* What do you know about reading these words? When you see the spelling *ar* in a word, try the sound /är/.

Mini-Lesson 1 — *R*-Controlled Vowel /är/ *ar*

Remind children that...

- Consonants and vowels may join together to spell a new sound.
- The letter *r* can change the way a vowel sounds.
- Many words contain the sound **/är/** spelled *ar.*

Word List

arm	mark
bark	part
far	start

Guide Practice

Use the routine above to teach children about the sound when *a* is followed by *r.* Today we will connect **/är/** with *ar* and blend words spelled with *ar.*

Write *barn.* Point to the letters *ar.* The letters *ar* spell the sound /är/. Let's blend the word together. As you run your hand under *barn,* say each sound slowly: /b//är//n/. Tell children to say the sounds of the word to themselves.

Now say the sounds quickly to say the word. What's the word? Yes, it's *barn.* Repeat the procedure with the remaining words.

barn   cart   dark   hard

If... children have difficulty reading words with /är/, **then...** have them use sound-by-sound blending (Routine Card 1) and whole-word blending (Routine Card 2) for decodable words.

On Their Own For additional practice, use the Word List and Worktext p. 38. Remind children that when they see the letters *ar* together in a word, they should try the sound /är/. Suggest that they look for these words as they read.

 **2** **R-Controlled Vowels /ôr/** *or, ore, oar*

Remind children that...
- The letter *r* can change the way a vowel sounds.
- Many words contain the sound **/ôr/** spelled *or, ore, oar.*

Word List

north	store	roar
sport	core	soap

Guide Practice

Use the routine on the previous page to teach children words with **/ôr/.** Today we will learn how to read and spell words with **/ôr/,** which can be spelled *or, ore,* and *oar.*

Write *or, ore,* and *oar.* Have children say /ôr/ several times as you point to *or, ore,* and *oar.* Then write *fort.* This is how I blend this word. Point to each sound-spelling as you say its sound: /f//ôr//t/. Then run your hand under *fort* as you blend the whole word. Have children practice saying the word without pausing between sounds. Follow this

procedure with the other words below to introduce *ore* and *oar* spellings.

fort	**more**	**snore**	**soar**

If... children have difficulty reading the words, **then...** use Routine Cards 1 and 7 to help them segment sounds and recognize the letter combinations that can spell /ôr/.

On Their Own See Worktext p. 39 and the Word List for additional practice. Help children spell each word with letter tiles. Then model blending sounds quickly to say each word.

3 **R-Controlled Vowels /ėr/** *er, ir, ur*

Remind children that...
- The letter *r* can change the way a vowel sounds.
- Many words contain the sound **/ėr/** spelled *er, ir,* or *ur.*

Word List

herd	dirt	burn
clerk	first	fur

Guide Practice

Remind children that the letter *r* can affect the way a vowel sounds. Today we will learn how to read and spell words with the sound **/ėr/.** Write *er, ir,* and *ur.* The sound /ėr/ can be spelled *er, ir,* or *ur.* Have children say /ėr/ as you point to these letter combinations. Next, write *germ.* This word has the letters *er,* and they spell the sound /ėr/. Listen to how I blend this word. Point to each sound-spelling as you say its sound: /j//ėr//m/. Have children blend the word with you. Follow this procedure to practice the *ir* and *ur* spellings in the remaining words.

germ	bird	girl	hurt	turn

If... children have difficulty reading the words, **then...** point to the *er, ir,* or *ur* in a word as you say the sound /ėr/.

On Their Own For additional practice with this sound-spelling, use Worktext p. 40 and the Word List. Provide letter tiles and use Routine Card 2 to model blending each word.

Vowel Digraphs (Long *e* and *a*)

Objectives:

- Teach concept of vowel digraphs.
- Introduce /ē/ spelled *ee.*
- Introduce /ē/ spelled *ea.*
- Introduce /ā/ spelled *ai, ay.*

MATERIALS

- Worktext pp. 41–43
- Routine Cards 2, 7
- Letter tiles

Set the scene Remind children that long vowel sounds can be spelled different ways. For example, you have learned that /ē/ can be spelled with the letters *e, y,* and *e_e.* You have also learned that /ā/ can be spelled with *a* and *a_e.* In this lesson, you will learn that the **long e** and **long a** sounds can also be spelled with other letters.

Routine **1. Connect Sound to Spelling** Connect this lesson to previously learned sound-spellings. Write *be, lucky,* and *these.* Read each word aloud, emphasizing the /ē/ sound in each as you point to the *e, y,* and *e_e.* What do you know about the vowel sounds in these words? (They have the sound /ē/.) Today we will learn to spell and read words with the sound /ē/ spelled *ee* and *ea.*

2. Model and Give Examples Use letter tiles or write *ee.* Have children say /ē/ several times as you point to *ee.* The letters *ee* spell the sound /ē/ as in the word *need.* Write *need* and have children say it aloud with you. Repeat with *ea* as in the word *mean.*

3. Model Blending *Need* has the letters *ee* (point to them), which spell the long *e* sound, /ē/. This is how I blend this word. Point to the letters as you say each sound. Then run your hand under *need* as you blend the whole word: /n//ē//d/, *need.* Follow this procedure to model *mean.* What do you know about reading these words? When you see the spelling *ee* or *ea* in a word, try the sound /ē/.

Mini-Lesson 1 — Long *e* (spelled *ee*)

Remind children that…

- Long vowel sounds can be spelled different ways.
- Many words contain /ē/ spelled *ee.*

Word List

deep	seen
feet	sleep
keep	

Guide Practice

Use step 3 of the routine above to help children connect /ē/ with *ee* and to blend long *e* words. Write *bee.* Have children say /ē/ several times as you point to *ee.* Then point to each sound-spelling as you say its sound: /b//ē/. Have children say the sounds quickly with you to say the word. What's the word? Yes, it's *bee.* Repeat the procedure with the remaining words below. Remind children to say the sounds quickly without pausing between sounds.

bee   feel   seed   tree

If… children have difficulty reading words with /ē/ spelled *ee,*

then… stretch the sounds in each word as you say them and run your hand below the word as children blend the sounds with you.

On Their Own For additional practice, use the Word List and Worktext p. 41. Remind children that when they see the letters *ee* together in a word, they should try the sound /ē/. Suggest that they look for these words as they read.

Mini-Lesson 2 Long *e* (spelled *ea*)

Remind children that...
- Long vowel sounds can be spelled different ways.
- Many words contain the sound /ē/ spelled *ea*.

Word List

eat	sneak
neat	steam
seat	

Guide Practice

Today we will learn that the letters *ea* can also spell the sound /ē/. Write *ea*. Have children say /ē/ several times as you point to *ea*. Then write *beat*. Use step 3 of the routine to blend the word. Point to each sound-spelling as you say its sound: /b//ē//t/. Then run your hand under *beat* as you blend the whole word. Have children practice saying the word several times without pausing between sounds. Follow this procedure with the remaining words below. When you see the letters *ea* in a word, try the sound /ē/.

beat	clean	heat	sea

If... children cannot read the words,
then... use Routine Cards 2 and 7 to help them segment sounds. Stretch the sounds as you say them.

On Their Own See Worktext p. 42 and the Word List for additional practice. Use each word in a sentence. Then help children spell each word with letter tiles. Model how to say the sounds without stopping between them.

Mini-Lesson 3 Long *a* (spelled *ai, ay*)

Remind children that...
- Long vowel sounds can be spelled different ways.
- Many words contain the sound /ā/ spelled *ai* and *ay*.

Word List

mail	say
rain	way
train	

Guide Practice

Remind children that the sound /ā/ can be spelled with *a,* as in *May.* This same long a sound can also be spelled *ai.* Write *ai* and *ay* and have children say /ā/ as you point to the letters. Today we will learn how to read and spell words with the sound /ā/ spelled *ai* and *ay.* Write *main.* The letters *ai* spell the sound /ā/ as in the word *main.* Listen as I blend this word. Point to each spelling as you say the sound: /m//ā//n/. Have children

blend the word with you. Repeat with *ay* as in the word *pay.* Follow the procedure to model the other words below.

main	tail	wait	pay	stay

If... children have difficulty reading the words,
then... point to the letters *ai* and *ay* and have students repeat the long a sound with you.

On Their Own For additional practice with /ā/ spelled *ai* and *ay*, use Worktext p. 43 and the Word List. Have children spell each word with letter tiles.

Vowel Digraphs (Long *o* and *i*)

Objectives:
- Teach concept of vowel digraphs.
- Introduce /ō/ spelled *ow.*
- Introduce /ō/ spelled *oa.*
- Introduce /ī/ spelled *ie, igh.*

MATERIALS
- Worktext pp. 44–46
- Routine Cards 2, 5
- Letter tiles

Set the scene Remind children that long vowel sounds can be spelled different ways. Explain that they have learned that /ō/ can be spelled with the letters *o* and *o_e* and that /ī/ can be spelled with the letters *i* and *i_e.* Now we will learn to spell the **long o and i** sounds in other ways.

Routine **1. Connect Sound to Spelling** To connect today's lesson to previously learned sound-spellings, write *go* and *nose.* Have children say them with you. What do you know about the vowel sounds in these words? (They have the long *o* sound: /ō/. *Go* has /ō/ spelled *o; nose* has /ō/ spelled *o_e.*) Today we will learn to spell and read words with the sound /ō/ spelled *ow.*

2. Model and Give Examples Write *ow.* Point to *ow.* The sound /ō/ can be spelled *ow.* Have children say /ō/ several times. The letters *ow* spell the sound /ō/ as in the word *low.* Repeat for *ow* as in the word *show.*

3. Model Blending Write *low.* This word has the letters *ow.* Point to them. These letters spell the long o sound, /ō/. This is how I blend this word. Point to each spelling as you say its sound. Then run your hand under *low* as you blend the whole word: /l//ō/, *low.* Have children say the word several times, without pausing between sounds. Follow this procedure to model *show.*

Mini-Lesson 1 — Long o (spelled *ow*)

Remind children that...
- Long vowel sounds can be spelled different ways.
- Many words contain the sound /ō/ spelled *ow.*

Word List

bowl	slow
crow	throw
row	

Guide Practice

Use step 3 of the routine above to help children read words with the **long o** sound spelled **ow.** Write *blow.* Have children say /ō/ several times with you as you point to the letters *ow.* Point to each spelling as you say its sound. This is how I blend this word. Run your hand under *blow* as you blend the whole word: /b//l//ō/. Then ask children to blend it with you. When you see the spelling *ow* in a word, try the sound /ō/.

Repeat with the remaining words.

blow	flow	grow
know	own	snow

If... children cannot read a word,

then... have them say the sounds as you touch the letter(s). Help them blend the sounds without stopping between them (Routine Card 2).

On Their Own For additional practice, use the Word List and Worktext p. 44. Help children use letter tiles to spell the word. Remind them to say the sounds to themselves before they read a word.

 **Mini-Lesson 2** **Long o (spelled *oa*)**

Remind children that...
- Long vowel sounds can be spelled different ways.
- Many words contain the sound /ō/ spelled *oa.*

Word List

boat	goat
coach	road
goal	soak

Guide Practice
Today we will learn that the letters *oa* can also spell the sound /ō/. Write *oa.* Have children say /ō/ with you several times as you point to *oa.* Then use letter tiles or write *coat.* What do you know about reading this word? Point to *oa.* When you see the spelling *oa* in a word, try the sound /ō/. Run your hand under each sound-spelling as you blend the whole word: /k//ō//t/, *coat.* Repeat the procedure with the remaining words.

coat	float	groan
soap	throat	toast

If... children have difficulty blending sounds, **then...** have them say the sounds in their heads before reading the word aloud together. Use the fluent reading routine (Routine Card 5) to help them read each word quickly and smoothly.

On Their Own See Worktext p. 45 and the Word List for additional practice. Provide children with letter tiles and have them spell each word. Ask children to take turns reading a word and using it in a sentence.

Mini-Lesson 3 **Long i (spelled *ie, igh*)**

Remind children that...
- Long vowel sounds can be spelled different ways.
- Many words contain the sound /ī/ spelled *ie* and *igh.*

Word List

lie	might
tie	sigh
light	tight

Guide Practice
Remind children that the long *i* sound has different spellings. Write *hi, my,* and *nice.* Point to the spellings for /ī/ in each word. Today we're going to learn that the sound /ī/ can also be spelled *ie* and *igh.* Write *ie.* Have children say /i/ as you point to *ie.* Then write *die.* This is how I blend this word. Point to each spelling as you say its sound. Then say the whole word: /d//ī/, *die.* Follow this procedure to model the long *i* sound spelled *igh*

as in *bright.* Continue the process to blend each of the remaining words below.

die	pie	bright
flight	high	sight

If... children have difficulty with /ī/ spelled *ie* and *igh,* **then...** draw a circle around the letters *ie* or *igh* in the word and say the long *i* sound. Model blending each word as you point to each sound-spelling.

On Their Own For additional practice, use Worktext p. 46. Have children use letter tiles to build and read the Word List words.

Phonics and Decoding Lesson 16
More Vowel Sounds

Objectives:
- Introduce short *e* spelled *ea*.
- Introduce /ù/ spelled *oo*.
- Introduce long *e* spelled *ie, ey*.

MATERIALS
- Worktext pp. 47–49
- Routine Cards 2, 7, 8
- Letter tiles

Set the scene Remind children that vowel sounds can be spelled different ways. You learned that the long *e* sound, /ē/, can be spelled with the letters *ea* or *ee*. Today we will learn to read words with the short *e* sound spelled *ea*, the /ù/ sound spelled *oo*, and the long *e* sound spelled *ie* and *ey*.

Routine

1. Connect Sound to Spelling Connect today's lesson to previously learned sound-spellings. Write *dream* and *seat*. What do you know about the vowel sound in these words? (The vowel is long; it says its name. *Dream* and *seat* have long *e* spelled *ea*.) Today you will learn to spell and read words with the short *e* sound, /e/, spelled *ea*.

2. Model and Give Examples Write and point to the letters *ea*. The short /e/ sound can be spelled *ea*. Have children say /e/ several times as you point to *ea*.

3. Model Blending Write *dead*. I see that this word has the letters *ea*. Point to them. They spell the /e/ sound. This is how I blend this word. Point to each spelling as you say its sound. Then run your hand under *dead* as you blend the whole word: /d//e//d/, *dead*. Have children say the word several times, without pausing between sounds. Follow this procedure to model *deaf*. When you see the spelling *ea* in a word, try the short *e* sound /e/.

Mini-Lesson 1 — Sound /e/ spelled *ea*

Remind children that...
- Vowel sounds can be spelled different ways.
- Many words contain the short *e* sound /e/ spelled *ea*.

Word List
heavy	sweat
spread	threat
steady	

Guide Practice
Use step 3 of the routine above to help children read words with the **/e/** sound spelled **ea.** Write *bread*. Notice this word has the letters *ea*. Point to the letters and have children repeat /e/ with you. Listen to how I blend this word. Run your hand under each sound-spelling in *bread* as you blend the whole word: /b//r//e//d/, *bread*. Then ask children to say it with you. Repeat this process with the other words below. Remember that the letters *ea* spell the sound /e/ in many words.

bread	breath	head	ready

If... children cannot read a word,
then... use whole-word blending (Routine Card 2) for decodable words. Say each word, use it in a sentence, and then have children repeat the word with you.

On Their Own For additional practice, use the Word List and Worktext p. 47. Help children use letter tiles to spell each word. Point to the letters *ea*. What is the sound for those letters? Yes, it is /e/.

 **2** **Sound /u̇/ spelled *oo***

Remind children that...
- Vowel sounds can be spelled different ways.
- Many words contain the sound /u̇/ spelled *oo*.

Word List

cook	hook
foot	shook
hood	

Guide Practice
Today we will learn that the letters *oo* can sometimes spell the sound /u̇/, as in *book*. Write *oo*. Have children say /u̇/ with you as you point to *oo*. Then write *book*. The letters *oo* spell the sound /u̇/ as in the word *book*. Listen as I blend this word. Point to each spelling as you say the sound. Then run your hand under *book* as you blend the whole word: /b//u̇//k/, book. Have children blend with and without you. Repeat the procedure with the remaining words.

book	good	look	took	wood

If... children have difficulty reading words,
then... have them say the sounds in their heads before reading the word aloud.

On Their Own See Worktext p. 48 and the Word List for additional practice. Ask children to take turns using each word in a sentence.

Mini-Lesson 3 **Sound /ē/ spelled *ie, ey***

Remind children that...
- Vowel sounds can be spelled different ways.
- Many words contain the long *e* sound /ē/ spelled *ie, ey*.

Word List

brief	donkey
grief	key
piece	valley

Guide Practice
Remind children that the long *e* sound has different spellings. Write *she, seat,* and *three*. Point to the letter(s) *e, ea,* and *ee*. The long *e* sound can be spelled *e* as in *she, ea* as in *seat,* and *ee* as in *three*. Today we will learn to read words that have the **long *e*** sound spelled *ie* and *ey*. Write *ie*. Have children say /ē/ as you point to *ie*. Then write *chief*. Point to each sound-spelling as you blend its sounds: /ch//ē//f/, *chief*. Have children blend the whole word. Follow this procedure for *ey,* as in the word *honey*.

Then continue the process to read the remaining words below. When you see the spellings *ie* and *ey,* try the sound /ē/.

chief	field	honey
monkey	key	

If... children cannot read the words,
then... exaggerate the /ē/ sound as you model blending each word several times.

On Their Own For additional practice, use Worktext p. 49 and the Word List. Say the sounds to yourself before saying the word aloud.

Vowel Patterns with /ü/

Objectives:
- Introduce /ü/ spelled *oo.*
- Introduce /ü/ spelled *ew.*
- Introduce /ü/ spelled *ue, ui.*

MATERIALS
- Worktext pp. 50–52
- Routine Cards 2, 7, 8
- Letter tiles

Set the scene Remind children that vowel sounds can be spelled in more than one way. For example, you have learned that /ī/ can be spelled with the letters *i, ie,* and *igh.* In this lesson, we will learn that the sound /ü/ can be spelled with *oo, ew, ue,* and *ui.*

Routine **1. Connect Sound to Spelling** Connect today's lesson to previously learned sound-spellings. Write *nine, pie,* and *high.* Have children say the words with you. What do you know about the vowel sounds in these words? (They have the long *i* sound: /ī/, spelled *i_e* in *nine, ie* in *pie,* and *igh* in *high.*) Today we will learn to connect the /ü/ sound, as in *moon,* with *oo* and to blend words with this sound.

2. Model and Give Examples Write and point to the letters *oo.* The sound /ü/ can be spelled *oo.* Have children say /ü/ several times as you point to *oo.* The letters *oo* spell the sound /ü/ as in the word *moon.*

3. Model Blending Write *moon.* I see that this word has the letters *oo* (point to them), which spell the /ü/ sound. This is how I blend this word. Point to each spelling as you say its sound. Then run your hand under *moon* as you blend the whole word: /m//ü//n/, *moon.* Have children say the word several times, without pausing between sounds. Follow this procedure to model *tool.*

Mini-Lesson 1 Sound /ü/ spelled *oo*

Remind children that...
- Vowel sounds can be spelled different ways.
- Many words contain the sound /ü/ spelled *oo.*

Word List
choose	room
goose	soon
pool	zoo

Guide Practice
Use step 3 of the routine above to help children read words with the /ü/ sound spelled *oo.* Write *broom.*

Have children say /ü/ several times with you as you point to the letters *oo.* Listen to how I blend this word. Run your hand under each sound-spelling in *broom* as you blend the whole word: /b//r//ü//m/, *broom.* Then ask children to say it with you. Continue this process with the other words below. Remind children that the letters *oo* spell the sound /ü/ in many words.

broom	**cool**	**shoot**	**spoon**	**tooth**

If... children cannot read a word,

then... use whole-word blending (Routine Card 2) for decodable words. Encourage children to say the sounds to themselves before they try to read the words aloud.

On Their Own For additional practice, use the Word List and Worktext p. 50. Help children use letter tiles to spell each word. Model blending each word and then ask children to blend it with you.

 **Sound /ü/ spelled *ew***

Remind children that...
- Vowel sounds can be spelled different ways.
- Many words contain the sound /ü/ spelled *ew.*

Word List

blew	flew
dew	knew
drew	

Guide Practice

You learned that the sound /ü/ can be spelled *oo*, as in *moon.* Today we will learn that the letters *ew* can also spell the sound **/ü/.** Write *ew.* Have children say /ü/ with you several times as you point to *ew.* Then use letter tiles or write *chew.* The letters *ew* spell the sound /ü/ as in the word *chew.* Listen as I blend this word. Point to each spelling as you say the sound. Then run your hand under *chew* as you blend the whole word: /ch//ü/, *chew.*

Have children blend with and without you. Repeat the procedure with the remaining words
chew   grew   new   stew

If... children have difficulty reading words,
then... have them say the sounds in their heads before reading the word aloud.

On Their Own See Worktext p. 51 and the Word List for additional practice. Ask children to take turns using each word in a sentence.

Mini-Lesson 3 **Sound /ü/ spelled *ue, ui***

Remind children that...
- Vowel sounds can be spelled different ways.
- Many words contain the sound /ü/ spelled *ue* and *ui.*

Word List

clue	bruise
cruel	suit
due	

Guide Practice

Remind children that the /ü/ sound has different spellings. Write *soon* and *knew.* Point to the sound /ü/ and its spellings in each word. You've been listening to words with the sound /ü/. Today we're going to learn that the sound **/ü/** can also be spelled *ue* and *ui.* Write *ue.* Have children say /ü/ as you point to *ue.* Then write *blue.* Point to each sound-spelling as you say its sound: /b//l//ü/. Run your hand under *blue* as you have children blend the whole word several times: /b//l//ü/, *blue.* Follow this

procedure for *ui*, as in the word *fruit.* Then continue the process to blend each of the remaining words below.
blue   glue   true   fruit   juice

If... children have difficulty with /ü/ spelled *ue* and *ui*,
then... exaggerate the /ü/ sound as you model blending each word several times.

On Their Own For additional practice, use Worktext p. 52. Have children use letter tiles to build the Word List words. Help them use each word in a sentence.

Vowel Diphthongs

Objectives:
- Teach concept of diphthongs.
- Introduce **/ou/** spelled *ou*.
- Introduce **/ou/** spelled *ow*.
- Introduce **/oi/** spelled *oi, oy.*

MATERIALS
- Worktext pp. 53–55
- Routine Cards 1, 2
- Letter tiles

Set the scene Remind children that vowel sounds can be spelled in more than one way. You learned that the sounds /ü/ and /ù/ can be spelled with the letters *oo.* In this lesson, we will learn to read words with the **/ou/** sound spelled *ou* and *ow* and the **/oi/** sound spelled *oi* and *oy.*

Routine

1. Connect Sound to Spelling Connect today's lesson to previously learned sound-spellings. Write *moon* and *book* and say them aloud. What do you know about the vowel sounds in these words? (In *moon,* they stand for the sound /ü/. In *book,* they stand for the sound /ù/.) Today you'll learn to spell and read words with the sound /ou/ spelled *ou,* as in *loud.*

2. Model and Give Examples Use letter tiles or write *ou.* The sound /ou/ can be spelled *ou.* Have children say /ou/ several times as you point to *ou.* The letters *ou* can spell the sound /ou/.

3. Model Blending Write *loud.* Do you see that this word has the letters *ou*? Point to them. They spell the sound /ou/. Point to the letters *ou* as children say /ou/ with you. This is how I blend this word. Point to each spelling as you say its sound: /l//ou//d/, *loud.* Run your hand under *loud* as you blend the whole word several times. What do you know about reading this word? When you see the spelling *ou* in a word, try the sound /ou/.

Mini-Lesson 1 Vowel Diphthong /ou/ *ou*

Remind children that...
- Vowel sounds can be spelled in more than one way.
- Many words contain the sound **/ou/** spelled *ou.*

Word List

cloud	proud
mouth	round
out	

Guide Practice
Use the routine above to help children connect /ou/ with *ou* and to blend words with this sound. Write *house.* Point to the letters *ou.* The letters *ou* spell the sound /ou/. Let's blend the word together. As you run your hand under *house,* say each sound slowly: /h//ou//s/. Model blending the word and then ask children to blend it with you. What's the word? Yes, it's *house.* Repeat the procedure

with the remaining words. Help children blend the sounds quickly, without pausing between sounds.

house	mouse	shout	sound

If... children have difficulty reading the words,
then... use whole-word blending (Routine Card 2) for decodable words. Remind children to say the sounds to themselves as they read each word.

On Their Own For additional practice, use the Word List and Worktext p. 53. Remind children that when they see the letters *ou* together in a word, they should try the sound /ou/. Suggest that they look for these words as they read.

 **Vowel Diphthong /ou/ *ow***

Remind children that...
- Vowel sounds can be spelled in more than one way.
- Many words contain the sound **/ou/** spelled *ow.*

Word List
cow	howl
crowd	now
frown	

Guide Practice
Today we will learn that the letters *ow* can also spell the sound /ou/. Write *ow.* Have children say /ou/ several times as you point to *ow.* Then write *brown.* Use step 3 of the routine to blend the word. Point to each sound-spelling as you say its sound: /b//r//ou//n/. Then run your hand under *brown* as you blend the whole word. Have children practice saying the word several times without pausing between sounds. Follow this procedure with the remaining words below.

brown   clown   growl   how   town

If... children cannot read the words,
then... use Routine Card 1 to help them identify sound-spellings. Have children say the sound as you touch the letter(s).

On Their Own See Worktext p. 54 and the Word List for additional practice. Use each word in a sentence. Then help children spell each word with letter tiles. Model blending sounds quickly and offer corrective feedback as needed. Remember to look for words with /ou/ spelled *ow* as you read.

Mini-Lesson 3 **Vowel Diphthong /oi/ *oi, oy***

Remind children that...
- Vowel sounds can be spelled in more than one way.
- Many words contain the sound **/oi/** spelled *oi* or *oy.*

Word List
choice	joy
noisy	toy
voice	

Guide Practice
Today we will learn that the vowel sound **/oi/** can be spelled with the letters *oi* and *oy.* Write *oi* and have children say /oi/ several times as you point to the letters. Write *boil.* I see that this word has the vowel letters *oi* (point to them). They can spell the sound /oi/. This is how I blend this word. Point to each spelling as you say its sound. Then run your hand under *boil* as you blend the whole word: /b//oi//l/. Have children blend the word with you several times. Follow the same procedure to introduce /oi/ spelled *oy* and to read the remaining words below.

boil   coin   point   boy   enjoy

If... children have difficulty reading the words,
then... point to each spelling and have children say its sound with you. Model how to blend the sounds quickly.

On Their Own For additional practice with /oi/ spelled *oi* and *oy,* use Worktext p. 55 and the Word List. Have children spell each word with letter tiles. Monitor their work and provide feedback.

Vowel Patterns with /ȯ/

Objectives:
- Introduce /ȯ/ spelled *a, al.*
- Introduce /ȯ/ spelled *ou, aw.*
- Introduce /ȯ/ spelled *augh, ough.*

MATERIALS
- Worktext pp. 56–58
- Routine Cards 2, 7, 8
- Letter tiles

Set the scene Remind children that vowel sounds can be spelled in different ways. You learned that /ā/ can be spelled with the letters *ai* and *ay*. Today we will learn that the sound /ȯ/ can be spelled in a number of different ways.

Routine **1. Connect Sound to Spelling** Connect today's lesson to previously learned sound-spellings. Write *pain* and *day.* Point to the vowels in each word. The vowel sound in these words is /ā/. *Pain* has /ā/ spelled *ai; day* has /ā/ spelled *ay.* Today we will learn to spell and read words with the sound /ȯ/ spelled *a* and *al.*

2. Model and Give Examples Write and point to the letter *a.* The sound /ȯ/ can be spelled *a.* Have children say /ȯ/ several times as you point to *a.* The letter *a* spells the sound /ȯ/ as in *ball.* Repeat this procedure for *al* as in *talk.*

3. Model Blending Write *ball.* I see that this word has the letter *a.* Point to it. The letter *a* spells the /ȯ/ sound. Listen as I blend this word. Point to each spelling as you say its sound. Then run your hand under *ball* as you blend the whole word: /b//ȯ//l/, *ball.* Have children say the word several times, without pausing between sounds. Follow this procedure to model *talk.* When you see the spelling *a* or *al,* try the sound /ȯ/.

Mini-Lesson 1

Sound /ȯ/ spelled *a, al*

Remind children that...
- Vowel sounds can be spelled different ways.
- Many words contain the sound /ȯ/ spelled *a, al.*

Word List

fall	bald
tall	halt
wall	

Guide Practice

Use step 3 of the routine above to help children connect /ȯ/ with *a* and *al* and to blend words with these sound-spellings. Write *call.* Point to *a.* Have children say /ȯ/ several times with you as you point to the *a.* Listen to how I blend this word. Run your hand under each sound-spelling in *call* as you say its sound: /k//ȯ//l/, *call.* Have children say *call* several times. Follow this procedure to model /ȯ/ spelled *al* as in *chalk* and to blend the remaining words.

call	fall	small
chalk	salt	walk

If... children cannot read a word,
then... use whole-word blending (Routine Card 2) for decodable words. Help children say and spell high-frequency words (Routine Card 8).

On Their Own For more practice, use Worktext p. 56 and the Word List. Help children use letter tiles to spell each word. Ask children to identify the sound /ȯ/ in each word before they read it aloud. Ask children to look for words with /ȯ/ spelled *a* and *al* as you read.

 **Mini-Lesson 2** **Sound /ȯ/ spelled *au, aw***

Remind children that...
- Vowel sounds can be spelled different ways.
- Many words contain the sound /ȯ/ spelled *au, aw.*

Word List

cause	jaw
haul	paw
draw	straw

Guide Practice

Explain that children learned that the sound /ȯ/ can be spelled *a* or *al* and that today they will learn that the letters *au* and *aw* can also spell the sound /ȯ/. Write *au.* Have children say /ȯ/ as you point to *au.* Write *fault.* The letters *au* spell the sound /ȯ/ as in the word *fault.* Listen as I blend this word. Point to each spelling as you say the sound. Run your hand under *fault* as you blend the whole word: /f//ȯ//l//t/, *fault.* Have children blend with you. Repeat the procedure to introduce /ȯ/ spelled *aw,* as in

crawl. Then continue to help children blend the remaining words.

fault	pause	sauce
crawl	hawk	yawn

If... children have difficulty reading words,
then... have them say the sounds in their heads before reading the word aloud. Use Routine Card 7 to help them connect /ȯ/ with *au* and *aw* spellings.

On Their Own See Worktext p. 57 and the Word List for additional practice. Help children take turns using each word in a sentence.

Mini-Lesson 3 **Sound /ȯ/ spelled *augh, ough***

Remind children that...
- Vowel sounds can be spelled different ways.
- Many words contain the sound /ȯ/ spelled *augh, ough.*

Word List

daughter	brought
naughty	ought
bought	

Guide Practice

Remind children that the /ȯ/ sound has different spellings. Write *all* and *paw.* Point to the letters that stand for /ȯ/ in each word. You've been listening to words with the sound /ȯ/. Today we will learn that the sound /ȯ/ can also be spelled *augh* and *ough.* Write *augh.* Have children say /ȯ/ as you point to *augh.* Then write *caught.* Point to each sound-spelling as you say its sound. Run your hand under *caught* as you have children blend the whole word several times: /k//ȯ//t/, *caught.* Follow this procedure for *ough,*

as in the word *fought.* Then continue the process to blend each of the remaining words below.

caught	taught	fought	thought

If... children cannot read these words,
then... exaggerate the /ȯ/ sound as you model blending each word several times.

On Their Own For additional practice, use Worktext p. 58. Have children use letter tiles to build the Word List words. Point to *augh* or *ough* in each word. When you see these letters, try the sound /ȯ/.

Schwa Sound and Silent Letters

Objectives:
- Teach concept of schwa sound **/ə/.**
- Teach concept of silent letters.
- Introduce words with the schwa sound in first and second syllables.
- Introduce words with **/n/** *gn* and **/s/** *st.*

MATERIALS
- Worktext pp. 59–61
- Routine Cards 1, 4
- Letter tiles

Set the scene Remind children that vowel sounds can be spelled different ways. In this lesson, we will learn the schwa sound, /ə/, can be spelled different ways. We will also learn to read words with the sound **/n/** spelled *gn* and the sound **/s/** spelled *st.*

Routine **1. Connect** Connect today's lesson to previous learning. You have learned to read words that have more than one syllable. Write *chilly* and *window.* Read the words: *chilly, window.* These words each have two syllables. Repeat the words. The first syllable is stressed, or accented.

2. Model and Give Examples Write *about.* This word has two syllables. Point to each syllable and say the word aloud: *a, bout, about.* Which syllable in *about* is accented? Yes, the second syllable is accented. Say *about* again, emphasizing the accented syllable. Point to the *a* in *about.* I notice the letter *a* in the first syllable. But I don't hear either the short *a* sound /a/ or the long *a* sound, /ā/. I hear the sound /ə/. This /ə/ sound is the schwa sound. Say it with me: /ə/.

3. Model Blending Point to *about* again. The schwa sound, /ə/, occurs in an unaccented syllable of *a* word. Point to the letter *a.* In *about,* the letter *a* spells the schwa sound. Model blending the whole word: /ə//b//ou//t/. Write *occur.* Have children read the word with you several times. Then repeat steps 2 and 3 to show children that in *occur,* the schwa sound, /ə/, is spelled with the letter *o.* The schwa sound can be spelled with different letters.

Mini-Lesson 1 Sound /ə/ in First Syllable

Remind children that...
- Vowel sounds can be spelled different ways.
- The vowel sound in an unaccented syllable is **/ə/,** the schwa sound.
- The sound /ə/ can be spelled different ways.
- Many words contain the schwa sound in the first syllable.

Word List

affect	supply
agree	support
around	

Guide Practice
Use step 3 of the routine above to help children read words that contain the schwa sound, **/ə/,** in the first syllable. Write the words below.

afraid	alarm	away
oppose	upon	

Read the first one, *afraid,* aloud. This word has two syllables: *a* and *fraid.* Which syllable is accented? Yes, the second syllable is accented. The first syllable has the schwa sound, /ə/. Say the word aloud, emphasizing the stressed syllable. The letter *a* spells the schwa sound in *afraid.* Repeat the procedure to help children identify the schwa sound in the other words. The schwa sound occurs in the first syllable of these words. It can be spelled by different letters. Point to each letter that spells the schwa sound.

If... children cannot read a word,
then... model blending the sounds aloud. Have children repeat after you.

On Their Own For more practice, use Worktext p. 59. Use letter tiles to help children build the Word List words. Have children point to each schwa sound.

 **Sound /ə/ in Second Syllable**

Remind children that...
- Vowel sounds can be spelled different ways.
- The vowel sound in an unaccented syllable is **/ə/,** the schwa sound.
- The sound /ə/ can be spelled different ways.
- Many words contain the schwa sound in the second syllable.

Word List

bacon	doctor
children	given
circus	robin

Guide Practice
Explain that today children will learn to read words that contain the schwa sound, **/ə/,** in the second syllable. Write *cabin.* Read it aloud. Cabin has two syllables: *cab, in.* Point to *cab.* The first syllable is accented. Point to *in.* The second syllable is unaccented. Have children say *cabin* with you. The letter *i* in the second syllable (point to *i*), stands for the sound /ə/, the schwa sound. Run your hand under the word and blend the whole word. Then write the other words below. Repeat the procedure to help children read the words. Run your hand under the unaccented syllable in each word and point to the vowel that spells the schwa sound.

cabin   even   pencil   pretzel   sofa

If... children cannot read a word,
then... help them break the words into syllables (Routine Card 4). Say each word, emphasizing the accented syllable. Have children read with you.

On Their Own See Worktext p. 60 and the Word List for additional practice. Ask children to point to the sound /ə/ in each word.

Mini-Lesson 3 **Silent Letters (/n/ spelled *gn* and /s/ spelled *st*)**

Remind children that...
- Sounds can be spelled different ways.
- Some letters can be silent.
- Many words contain the sounds **/n/** spelled **gn** and **/s/** spelled **st.**

Word List

design	hustle
gnat	moisten
fasten	

Guide Practice
Write *net* and *sip.* Read them aloud. You have studied words with the sounds /n/ and /s/. Today you'll learn to spell and read words with /**n**/ spelled *gn* and /**s**/ spelled *st.* Write *gnome.* Point to the letters *gn.* This word has the letters *gn.* They spell the sound /n/. This is how I blend this word. Point to each spelling as you blend the whole word: /n//ō//m/. Follow this procedure to introduce the sound /s/ spelled *st.* Model blending the other words below. When you see the letters *gn* in these words, they spell the sound /n/. The *g* is silent. When you see the letters *st* in these words, they spell the sound /s/. The *t* is silent.

gnome	sign	resign
castle	listen	whistle

If... children cannot read the words,
then... use Routine Card 1 to model blending each sound.

On Their Own For additional practice, use Worktext p. 61 and the Word List. Run your hand under each sound-spelling as you have children blend the word.

Phonics and Decoding Lesson 21
More Silent Letters

Objectives:
- Teach concept of silent letters.
- Introduce /n/ spelled **kn.**
- Introduce /r/ spelled **wr.**
- Introduce /m/ spelled **mb.**

MATERIALS
- Worktext pp. 62–64
- Routine Card 1, 2, 7
- Letter tiles

Set the scene
Remind children that sounds can be spelled different ways. Explain that in some words not every letter has a sound. In this lesson, we will learn about words that include letters that are silent. For instance, we will read and say words that begin with **kn.** In these words, the *k* does not stand for the sound **/k/.** The *k* is silent.

Routine

1. Connect Sound to Spelling Connect this lesson to previously learned sound-spellings. Write *gnome* and *gnat.* Ask children what they know about the beginning sounds in these words. (They both begin with the sound /n/ spelled *gn.*) You have heard words with the sound /n/. Today you'll learn to spell and read words with the sound /n/ spelled *kn.*

2. Model and Give Examples Use letter tiles or write *kn.* The sound /n/ can be spelled *kn.* Have children say /n/ several times as you point to *kn.* The letters *kn* spell the sound /n/. The *k* is silent.

3. Model Blending Write *knee.* This word begins with the letters *kn.* They spell the sound /n/. Point to the letters *kn* as children say /n/ with you. This is how I blend this word. Point to each spelling as you say its sound: /n//ē/. Run your hand under *knee* as you blend the whole word several times. Follow this procedure to model *knot.* What do you know about reading these words? When you see the spelling *kn* in a word, try the sound /n/. The *k* is silent.

Mini-Lesson 1 — Silent Letter /n/ Spelled *kn*

knife	knob	knock	know

Remind children that...
- Sounds can be spelled different ways.
- Some letters can be silent.
- Many words contain the sound **/n/** spelled **kn.**

Word List

kneel	known
knew	knows
knots	

Guide Practice
Use the routine above to help children connect **/n/** with **kn** and to blend words with this sound. Write *knife.* Point to the letters *kn.* The letters *kn* spell the sound /n/. Let's blend the word together. As you run your hand under *knife,* say each sound slowly: /n//ī//f/. Model blending the word and then ask children to blend it with you. What's the word? Yes, it's *knife.* Repeat the procedure with the remaining words.

If... children have difficulty reading words that begin with *kn,*

then... use whole-word blending (Routine Card 2) and remind children to say the sounds to themselves as they read each word.

On Their Own For additional practice, use the Word List and Worktext p. 62. Remind children that when they see the letters *kn* together in a word, they should try the sound /n/. Suggest that they look for these words as they read.

 **2 Silent Letter /r/ Spelled wr**

Remind children that...
- Sounds can be spelled different ways.
- Some letters can be silent.
- Many words contain the sound /r/ spelled **wr.**

Word List

wrapped	**writes**
wraps	**writing**
wreck	

Guide Practice

Today we will learn that the letters **wr** can also spell the sound **/r/.** Write *wr.* Have children say /r/ several times as you point to *wr.* Then write *wrote.* Use step 3 of the routine to blend the word. Point to each sound-spelling as you say its sound: /r/ō/t/. Then run your hand under *wrote* as you blend the whole word. Have children practice

saying the word several times without pausing between sounds. Follow this procedure with the remaining words below.

wrote   **wrist**   **write**   **wrong**

If... children cannot read the words,
then... use Routine Cards 1 and 7 to help them identify sound-spellings. Stretch the sounds as you say them.

On Their Own See Worktext p. 63 and the Word List for additional practice. Use each word in a sentence. Then help children spell each word with letter tiles. Model blending sounds quickly to say each word. When you see a word beginning with *wr,* try the sound /r/. The *w* is silent.

---

3 Silent Letter /m/ Spelled mb

Remind children that...
- Sounds can be spelled different ways.
- Some letters can be silent.
- Many words contain the sound /m/ spelled **mb.**

Word List

climb	**lambs**
combs	**lamb**
crumb	

Guide Practice

Remind children that the sound /m/ can be spelled *m,* as in *map.* It can also sometimes be spelled *mb.* Use letter tiles or write **mb** and have children say **/m/** as you point to the letters. Today we will learn how to read and spell words with the sound /m/ spelled *mb.* Write **comb.** The letters *mb* spell the sound /m/ as in the word *comb.* The *b* is silent. Listen as I blend this word. Point to each spelling as you say the sound: /k//ō//m/. Have children

blend the word with you several times. Follow this procedure with the remaining words.

comb   **dumb**   **lamb**   **thumb**

If... children have difficulty reading the words,
then... point to the *mb* in each word and remind them that the *b* is silent. Have children blend each word with you several times.

On Their Own For additional practice with /m/ spelled *mb,* use Worktext p. 64 and the Word List. Have children spell each word with letter tiles. Monitor their work and provide feedback.

More Syllable Patterns

Objectives:
- Introduce concept of syllable patterns.
- Introduce syllable pattern **C + *le.***
- Introduce syllable pattern **VCCCV.**
- Introduce syllable pattern **CV/VC.**

MATERIALS
- Worktext pp. 65–67
- Routine Cards 2, 4
- Letter tiles

Set the scene Remind children that some words can be broken into smaller word parts. You learned how to divide many words into syllables. Today we will learn how to divide words that contain three common syllable patterns.

Routine

1. Connect Connect today's lesson to previous learning. Write *begin* and *camel.* These are words you know. Point to the words and have children read them with you. These words can be broken into syllables. Point to each syllable. Today we will learn how to divide words that end with a consonant and the letters *le.*

2. Model and Give Examples Write *jungle.* Read the word aloud: *jungle. Jungle* can be divided into two syllables. Cover *gle* and read the first syllable aloud: *jun.* Then cover *jun* and read the last syllable aloud: *gle.* Finally, say the word together. *Jungle* has two syllables. In words like *jungle* that end with a consonant + *le,* the last syllable is made up of the consonant and *le.*

3. Model Blending Write *gentle.* When I see a word that ends with a consonant and *le,* I know to divide the word so that the consonant goes with the *le* to make a syllable. Point to the *le.* I read the syllables one after the other to say the word. In this word the syllables are *gen* and *tle.* Let's read it together: *gen, tle, gentle.* Repeat the process with *puzzle.* Remind children that the consonant and *le* form the final syllable.

Mini-Lesson 1 — Syllable Pattern C + *le*

Remind children that...
- Some words can be broken into smaller word parts.
- A syllable is a word part that contains a single vowel sound.
- Many words contain the syllable pattern **C + *le.***

Word List
apple	sample
ankle	simple
paddle	table

Guide Practice
Use step 3 of the routine above to help children divide and read words that end with the syllable pattern **C + *le.*** Write *bottle.* When you see a word that ends with a consonant plus *le,* you know how to divide the word into syllables. The consonant goes with the *le* to make a syllable. Point to the last three letters: *tle.* Let's read the syllables one after the other and say the word. In this word, the syllables are *bot* and *tle.* We read: *bot, tle, bottle.* Repeat the process for the other words below.

bottle	**little**	**puddle**	**title**	**uncle**

If... children cannot read a word,

then... use Routine Card 4 to help them identify its two syllables. Use Routine Card 2 to help children blend the word's sounds.

On Their Own For more practice, use Worktext p. 65 and the Word List. Have children use letter tiles to build each word. Monitor children as they break the words into syllables in order to read them.

 **Mini-Lesson 2** **Syllable Pattern VCCCV**

Remind children that...
- Some words can be broken into smaller word parts.
- A syllable is a word part that contains a single vowel sound.
- Many words contain the syllable pattern **VCCCV**.

Word List

address	instant
control	monster
explode	subtract

Guide Practice

Explain that today children will learn to divide words that have three consonants in the middle. Write and say *children*. *Children* has two syllables. Point to the three consonants in the middle of *children*. When I see a word with three consonants in the middle, I divide the word between the single consonant and the blend. I read the syllables one after the other to say the word. Cover *dren* and read the first syllable: *chil*. Then cover *chil* and read the second syllable: *dren*. The syllables are *chil* and *dren*. I read: *chil, dren, children*. Follow this procedure to help children divide each remaining word below into two syllables and read it.

children	complete	explain
hundred	surprise	

If... children have difficulty reading words,

then... have them identify one syllable at a time as you cover the remaining syllable.

On Their Own See Worktext p. 66 for additional practice. Help children break the Word List words into syllables and read them aloud.

Mini-Lesson 3 **Syllable Pattern CV/VC**

Remind students that ...
- Some words can be broken into smaller word parts.
- A syllable is a word part that contains a single vowel sound.
- Many words contain the syllable pattern **CV/VC**.

Word List

cruel	neon
diet	poet
liar	ruin

Guide Practice

Tell children that today they will learn how to divide words that have two vowels together when each one spells a different vowel sound. Write *giant*. Read the word aloud: *giant*. *Giant* has two syllables. Point to the vowels in *giant*. Explain that sometimes two vowels together make one vowel sound. In other words, the two vowels spell two separate vowel sounds. This happens because each vowel is in a different syllable. Point to *giant*. The syllables are *gi* and *ant*. I read: *gi, ant, giant*. When you see a word with two vowels together when each vowel stands for a different sound, divide the word between the vowels. Then read the syllables one after the other. Continue the process with the remaining words below.

giant	lion	poem	quiet	react

If... children cannot read a word,

then... run your hand under its syllables as you emphasize the two different vowel sounds.

On Their Own For more practice, use Worktext p. 67 and the Word List. Have children use letter tiles to build and read the words.

Prefixes and Suffixes

Objectives:
- Introduce prefixes *un-* and *re-*.
- Introduce suffixes *-er* and *-or*.
- Introduce suffixes *-ly* and *-ful*.

MATERIALS
- Worktext pp. 68–70
- Routine Cards 1, 4
- Letter tiles

Set the scene Remind children that many words can be broken into smaller parts. In this lesson, they will learn to read words that contain word parts that can be added at the beginnings or ends of words.

Routine

1. Connect Connect today's lesson to previous learning. Write and read *place* and *zip.* Today we will learn how to make and read new words by adding *re-* and *un-* at the beginning of these words and other words you know. These word parts are called *prefixes.*

2. Model and Give Examples Point to *place.* Let's add a prefix to make a new word. Add *re-* before *place.* This is how I read words with prefixes. Cover the prefix and read the base word: *place.* Then read the prefix: *re-.* Then I read the two parts from left to right to read the word: *re, place, replace.* Run your hand under *replace* as you say the word. The word part *re-* means "again." *Replace* means "to place again." Repeat this procedure to add the prefix *un-* before *zip.* Explain that the word part *un-* means "do the opposite of" or "not." Make sure children understand what *unzip* means.

3. Model Blending Point to *replace* again. *Replace* begins with the prefix *re-.* The prefix *re-* means "again." The base word *place* and the prefix *re-* make up the word *replace.* To read this word, read the prefix, read the base word, and then read the two parts together: *re, place, replace.* Repeat the procedure with *un-* and *unzip.* Encourage children to avoid pausing between the word parts as they read the word.

Mini-Lesson 1 — Prefixes *re-, un-*

Remind children that…
- Many words can be broken into smaller parts.
- Prefixes are word parts that are added at the beginning of a word.
- Many words begin with the prefixes *re-* and *un-*.

Word List

recycle	uncover
redo	unlucky
replay	unreal
reuse	untie

Guide Practice

Use step 3 of the routine above to help children read words that begin with the prefixes *re-* and *un-*. Write *refill. Refill* has two parts: the prefix *re-* and the base word *fill.* Explain that adding a prefix to a word changes its meaning. *Refill* means "to fill again." To read this word, read the base word first: *fill.* Next, read *re-.* Then read the parts from left to right: *re, fill, refill.* Have children read *refill* with you. Continue the procedure with the other words below.

refill	repay	reread
review	rewrite	

Repeat the procedure to introduce *un-* and read the following words.

unclear	unhappy	unlike
unpack	unwrap	

If… children cannot read a word,

then… use the word part strategy (Routine Card 4) to help them break the word into chunks. You may need to help them blend the base word before reading the whole word.

On Their Own For more practice, use Worktext p. 68 and the Word List. Use letter tiles to build prefixes and base words.

 **Mini-Lesson 2** **Suffixes -er, -or**

Remind children that...
- Many words can be broken into smaller parts.
- Suffixes are word parts that are added at the end of a word.
- Many words end with the suffixes **-er** and **-or.**

Word List

listener	collector
seller	inventor
worker	

Guide Practice

Explain to children that they learned that the prefixes *re-* and *un-* can be added to many words to make new words. Tell them that today they will learn that the word parts **-er** and **-or** can be added at the end of many words. Explain that a suffix is a word part that can be added at the end of a base word to make a new word. Write and say *play*. Add -er at the end. This word is *player*. It is made up of *play*, the base word, and -er, a suffix. The suffixes -er and -or mean "a person or thing that ___." For example, a player is a person who plays. Read the parts together: *play, er, player*. Write the remaining words below. Circle the suffixes. Then repeat the procedure with each word.

player	reporter	teacher
actor	sailor	visitor

If... children have difficulty reading words,

then... help them blend sounds in the base words and then add the suffixes.

On Their Own See Worktext p. 69 and the Word List for additional practice.

 **Mini-Lesson 3** **Suffixes -ly, -ful**

Remind children that...
- Many words can be broken into smaller parts.
- Suffixes are word parts that are added at the end of a word.
- Many words end with the suffixes **-ly** and **-ful.**

Word List

calmly	forgetful
gladly	peaceful
mainly	spoonful

Guide Practice

Remind children that suffixes are word parts added at the end of a base word. Today they will learn how to read and spell words with two new suffixes: **-ly** and **-ful.** Write and say *slow*. Add -ly. *Slowly* ends with -ly. It means "in a slow way." Model reading the base word, the suffix, and then the word parts together. Run your hand under the word as children say it with you: *slow, ly, slowly.* Repeat the procedure to introduce the suffix -ful in *careful*. *Careful* ends with -ful. It means "full of care." Continue the procedure with the remaining words.

slowly	sadly	tightly
careful	fearful	hopeful

If... children cannot read the words,

then... use whole-word blending to read the base word (Routine Card 1). Then remind children to read the base word and the suffix one after the other without pausing.

On Their Own For additional practice, use Worktext p. 70. Monitor children as they use letter tiles to build the base word and the suffixes of the Word List words.

Common Syllables and Multisyllabic Words

Objectives:
- Introduce common syllables *-tion, -sion.*
- Introduce common syllables *-ture.*
- Introduce multisyllabic words.

MATERIALS
- Worktext pp. 71–73
- Routine Cards 1, 2, 4
- Letter tiles

Set the scene Remind children that they have learned to read words that follow different syllable patterns. Today we will learn to read words that end with one of several common syllables and to read multisyllabic words.

Routine **1. Connect** Connect today's lesson to previous learning. Write *candle* and *purple.* These are words you know. They end in a syllable that is consonant plus *le.* Run your hand under the last syllable of each word. Today we will learn about syllables *-tion* and *-sion.*

2. Model and Give Examples Write and read aloud *action. Action* has two syllables. Cover *-tion* and read the first syllable aloud: *ac.* Then cover *ac* and read the second syllable aloud: *-tion.* Finally, say the word: *action. Action* is one of many words that ends with the syllable *-tion.* Repeat the process to introduce the syllable *-sion* in *mansion.*

3. Model Blending Write *section.* Point to the letters *-tion* at the end of the word. I know that these letters usually make up a word's last syllable. When I see a word that ends with the syllable *-tion,* I divide the word before these letters. I read the syllables one after the other to say the word. Point to *section.* In this word, the syllables are *sec* and *tion.* I read: *sec, tion, section.* Repeat the process with the syllable *-sion* in *tension.* Have children read the syllables one after the other quickly with and without you.

Mini-Lesson 1 — Syllables *-tion, -sion*

Remind children that...
- Many words can be broken into more than one syllable.
- Many words include common syllable patterns.
- Many words end with the common syllables *-tion, -sion.*

Word List

election	confusion
lotion	discussion
vacation	invasion

Guide Practice
Use step 3 of the routine above to help children read words that end with the common syllables *-tion* and *-sion.* Write *nation* and read it aloud. Point to the ending *-tion.* I know that these letters usually make up the last syllable of some words. When a word ends with *-tion,* divide the word just before these letters. Draw a line before the letter *t.* The word has two syllables: *na* and *tion.* Let's read the syllables one after the other: *na, tion, nation.* Repeat the procedure with the letters *-sion,* as in *confusion.* Help children divide each of the other words below into syllables. Continue the procedure to help children blend each word.

nation	question	station
mission	vision	

If... children cannot read a word,
then... use different colors to show different syllables and use whole-word blending (Routine Card 2) for decodable words.

On Their Own For more practice, use Worktext p. 71 and the Word List. Help children use letter tiles to break each word into syllables.

 **Syllable -ture**

Remind children that...
- Many words can be broken into more than one syllable.
- Many words include common syllable patterns.
- One common syllable is **-ture.**

Word List
creature   mature

feature   posture

lecture

Guide Practice
Explain that today children will learn to read words that end with the common syllable **-ture.** Write *capture* and read it aloud. *Capture* has two syllables. Cover *-ture* and read the first syllable aloud: *cap.* Then cover *cap* and read the second syllable aloud: *-ture.* Point to the ending *-ture.* These letters usually make up the last syllable. When I see a word that ends with the syllable *-ture,* I divide the word just before these letters. I read the syllables one

after the other. Point to the syllables *cap* and *ture* and read the word: *cap, ture, capture.* Follow this procedure with the remaining words below.

capture   future   nature

pasture   picture

If... children cannot read a word,

then... help them identify the word parts (Routine Card 4) and blend individual syllables before reading the whole word (Routine Card 1).

On Their Own See Worktext p. 72 and the Word List for additional practice. Ask children to take turns using each word in a sentence.

Mini-Lesson 3   Multisyllabic Words

Remind children that...
- Many words can be broken into more than one syllable.
- Many words include common syllable patterns.
- Recognize syllable patterns in multisyllabic words to make them easier to read.

Word List
confusion   remarkable

education   surroundings

furniture   untruthful

individual

Guide Practice
Tell children that today they will break apart words with three or more syllables to make them easier to read. Write *adventure.* I see a chunk at the beginning: *ad.* Point to *ad* and draw a line after it. I see that the word ends with the common syllable pattern *-ture.* Draw a line before the *t.* Say the word again: *adventure.* Point to and say the

middle part: *ven.* Point to and say the final part: *ture.* Say the chunks slowly: *ad ven ture.* Let's say the three parts quickly to say the whole world: *adventure.* Is it a real word? Yes, I know the word *adventure.* Continue the process to break the remaining words below into chunks to read them.

adventure   reappearing   location

signature   unacceptable

If... children cannot read the words,

then... identify and say one part at a time as you cover the remaining parts.

On Their Own For additional practice, use Worktext p. 73 and the Word List. Monitor children as they use letter tiles to break the words into smaller chunks.

Phonics and Decoding Lesson 25
More Endings

Objectives:
- Teach concept of inflected endings.
- Introduce endings *-er, -est.*
- Introduce endings *-ed, -ing* that require doubling the final consonant.
- Introduce endings *-ed, -ing* with silent *e* words.

MATERIALS
- Worktext pp. 74–76
- Routine Cards 1, 4
- Letter tiles

Set the scene Remind children that some words can be broken into smaller word parts. In this lesson, we will learn about words with endings *-er, -est, -ed,* and *-ing.*

Routine **1. Connect** Connect this lesson to previous learning. Write *pack, packed,* and *packing.* Read the words. These words have the endings *-ed* and *-ing.* Today we will learn how to make new words by adding the endings *-er* and *-est* to words you know.

2. Model and Give Examples Write and read *fast.* Add *-er.* We can add *-er* to the end of *fast* to make a new word. Cover the word part *-er* and read the base word: *fast.* Then cover the base word and read the word part *-er* aloud: /ər/. Say the new word: *faster.* Repeat the process to form *fastest* by adding the ending *-est.*

3. Model Blending When I see a word with *-er* at the end, I notice the two parts in the word. Point to the word part *-er* in *faster.* I read the parts one after the other to say the word. In this word, the parts are *fast* and *-er.* I read: *fast, er, faster.* Explain that we use the ending *-er* when we compare two things. Give an example: Sue runs faster than I do. Repeat with the ending *-est.* Have children read the word with you: *fast, est, fastest.* Explain that we use the ending *-est* when we compare three or more things. Give an example: Sue runs the fastest of all the girls.

Mini-Lesson 1 — Endings *-er, -est*

Remind children that...
- Many words can be broken into smaller word parts.
- Many words end with the word parts *-er* and *-est.*

Word List
shorter	shortest
softer	softest
taller	tallest

Guide Practice
Use steps 2 and 3 of the routine on the previous page to help children read words with endings *-er* and *-est.* Write *harder.* This word has two parts. The parts are *hard* and *-er.* When you see a base word with *-er* at the end, read the two parts one after the other to say the word: *hard, er, harder.* Have children say the word with you. Point out the double consonant if the word has one. Repeat the procedure with the other words below.

harder	longer	quicker	faster

Follow the procedure for the ending *-est* and the words below.

hardest	longest	quickest	fastest

If... children cannot read a word,
then... use Routine Card 4 to help them identify and read the word parts. Model using sound-by-sound blending to read the first syllable (Routine Card 1).

On Their Own For additional practice, use Worktext p. 74. For more practice with *-er* and *-est* endings, use the Word List. Use letter tiles to form the two parts of each word.

 **Mini-Lesson 2** **Endings -ed, -ing: Double Final Consonant**

Remind children that...
- Many words can be broken into smaller word parts.
- In many words the final consonant is doubled before the endings **-ed** and **-ing.**

Word List

jogged	jogging
petted	petting
skipped	skipping
stopped	stopping

Guide Practice

Tell children that they have learned to read words that have endings **-ed** and **-ing** added to them, such as *wished* and *wishing.* Today they will learn to read words that need spelling changes when they add these same endings to them. Write *clap* and *clapped.* Read the words aloud. Whenever I see a short vowel word that ends in just one consonant (point to *p* in *clap*), I know I have to double that consonant before I add the ending. *Clap* ends with one consonant: *p.* I double the *p* before I add the ending *-ed.* Point to *clapped.* Read it: *clap, ped, clapped.* Repeat with the other words below.

clapped	hopped	planned
rubbed	slipped	

Write *clapping.* Repeat the procedure with *-ing.* Model reading the words below.

clapping	hopping	planning
rubbing	slipping	

If... children cannot read a word,
then... cover the ending and have children read the base word. Then model reading one part after another without pausing.

On Their Own See Worktext p. 75 and the Word List for additional practice.

 **Mini-Lesson 3** **Endings -ed, -ing: Drop Silent e**

Remind children that...
- Many words can be broken into smaller word parts.
- In many words, such as *like* and *love,* the final *e* is silent.
- When you add **-ed** and **-ing** endings to words that end with silent *e,* drop the **e.**

Word List

hiked	hiking
moved	moving
raced	racing

Guide Practice

Explain to children that they can read many words with endings **-ed** and **–ing.** Today they'll learn how to add these endings to words that end with **silent e.** Write *bake.* *Bake* ends with silent *e.* To add *-ed* to a word that ends in silent *e,* drop the *e* before adding the ending. Erase the *e* and add *-ed.* Cover the ending *-ed.* Say the base word. Remind children that you dropped the *e* before you added the *-ed.* Cover the letters *bak* and read the ending *-ed* aloud: /t/. Read the word together: /b//ā//k/ + /t/, *baked.* Continue the procedure with the other words below.

baked	closed	hoped
saved	voted	

Repeat the procedure to help children read the words below with the *-ing* ending.

baking	closing	hoping
saving	voting	

If... children cannot read the words,
then... model blending the sounds and have children repeat after you.

On Their Own For additional practice, use Worktext p. 76 and the Word List. Form each base word with letter tiles. Then remove the *e* before adding the endings.

Plurals

Objectives:
- Teach concept of plurals.
- Introduce plural words that end in **-s** or **-es.**
- Introduce plural words that end in **-ves.**

MATERIALS
- Worktext pp. 77–79
- Routine Cards 2, 4, 8
- Letter tiles

Set the scene Tell children that they can read words such as *desk* and *class.* Remind them that these words are singular. Today they're going to learn how to make these words—and others like them—show "more than one." Also remind children that many words can be broken into smaller word parts. We will learn about adding different word parts to form plural words.

Routine

1. Connect Connect the lesson to previous learning. Write and read aloud *spot* and *rug.* Read the words. Today we will learn to make new words by adding -*s* to these words and other words you know.

2. Model and Give Examples Point to *spot.* We can add the word part -*s* to *spot* to make a new word that means "more than one." Add -*s.* Cover the -*s* and read the base word aloud: *spot.* Then cover the base word and read the word part -*s:* /s/. The final -*s* in *spots* spells the sound /s/. Have children say *spots* with you. S*pots* is a plural word. The plural form of *spot* is *spots,* which means more than one spot. Repeat the process to form the plural of *rug.*

3. Model Blending Tell students that when they see a word with -*s* at the end, they should cover the word part -*s* and read the word. Then they should read the -*s* and then read the whole word. Point to *spots.* Say: *spot, s, spots.* Point to the two parts in *rugs.* Read the parts to say the word: *rug, s, rugs.* Explain to students that the -*s* in *rugs* spells the sound /z/.

Mini-Lesson 1 Plural -*s*

Remind children that…
- Many words are made up of smaller word parts.
- Plural words refer to more than one person, place, thing, or idea.
- Many plural words end in **-s.**

Word List

elephants	mugs
flowers	numbers
mothers	villages

Guide Practice
Explain that today children will learn how to read words that use the word part **-s** to mean "more than one." Write *animal.* Run your hand under the syllables and say the word: *an i mal.* Add -*s.* When you see a word with -*s* at the end, you know to read the parts one after the other. Run your hand under *animal* and then the letter *s.* Have children say *animal, s, animals. Animals* is a plural word.

It means "more than one animal." Repeat the procedure with the other words below. Point out that the letter -*s* at the end of a plural word can sometimes stand for the sound /s/ and sometimes stand for the sound /z/.

animals	**friends**	**logs**
pieces	**thoughts**	

If… children cannot read a word,
then… break the word into parts and have children repeat them. Use Routine Card 8 to help children read and spell high-frequency words.

On Their Own See Worktext p. 77 and the Word List for additional practice. Help children build plural words with letter tiles.

Mini-Lesson 2 — Plural *-es*

Remind children that...
- Many words are made up of smaller word parts.
- Plural words refer to more than one person, place, thing, or idea.
- Many plural words end in *-es.*

Word List

bosses	patches
classes	foxes
catches	sixes

Guide Practice

You have learned to make and read plural words that end in *-s.* Today we will learn to make and read the plural forms of words that end with the letters *-s, -ch,* and *-x.* To make words plural that end with those letters, we add *-es.* Write and say *bus.* Circle the *-s.* This word ends in *-s.* We can add *-es* to the end of *bus* to make a plural word. Write *buses.* Point to the word part *-es.*

I notice the word part *-es.* I read the word and then read the word part: *bus, es, buses.* Repeat the procedure with the remaining words below.

buses	glasses	matches
watches	foxes	taxes

If... children cannot read a word,

then... use Routine Cards 2 and 4 to model blending sounds in the base word and identifying word parts.

On Their Own For additional practice, use Worktext p. 78. For more practice, use the Word List. Monitor children as they break the word into parts.

Mini-Lesson 3 — Plural *f* or *fe* to *v*

Remind children that...
- Many words are made up of smaller word parts.
- Plural words refer to more than one person, place, thing, or idea.
- Some plural words end in *-ves.*

Word List

calves/calf	lives/life
elves/elf	thieves/thief
halves/half	

Guide Practice

Remind children that they have learned to add *-s* or *-es* to form many plural words. Explain that today they will learn to read plural words that are formed by changing some letters at the end of singular words. Plural words are easier to read when you know their singular form. Write *knives.* Circle the letters *ves.* Plurals that end in the letters *ves* are often formed from words that end in *f* or *fe.* If I take away

the word part *-es* and change the *v* to *f* or *fe,* I can figure out the singular form. Model that process. Point to and say *knife.* You know *knife. Knives* is the plural form of *knife.* Follow this procedure to model the other word pairs.

knives/knife	leaves/leaf
shelves/shelf	wives/wife

If... children cannot read the words,

then... run your hand under each part as you say the word together.

On Their Own For additional practice, use Worktext p. 79 and the Word List. Use letter tiles to change each plural to its singular form.

Compound Words

Objectives:
- Teach concept of compound words.
- Introduce strategy for reading compound words.

MATERIALS
- Worktext pp. 80–82
- Routine Cards 2, 4
- Letter tiles

Set the scene Remind children that they have learned to put together word parts to make new words. You have learned to make new words by adding a word part to a word you know. Today you will learn to read **compound words**, words made up of two or more shorter words.

Routine **1. Connect** Connect today's lesson to previous learning. Write *tea* and *pot*. You know each of these words. Let's read them: *tea, pot.* In this lesson, we will learn how to make a new word by putting these words together to make a compound word.

2. Model and Give Examples Point to *tea* and *pot*. We can add *pot* to the end of *tea* to make a new word. Write *pot* at the end of *tea* to make *teapot*. Cover *pot* and read the first word part aloud: *tea.* Then cover *tea* and read the word part *pot* aloud: *pot.* Finally, read the new word: *teapot.*

3. Model Blending Point to the word parts *tea* and *pot*. I notice the two parts in the word. I read the parts one after the other to say the word. In this word the parts are *tea* and *pot*. Have children read the word with you: *tea, pot, teapot.* Then write *backpack*. Repeat the procedure to help children identify the two word parts in *backpack*. Have them read the word with you several times: *back, pack, backpack.* Remind children that when they see a compound word, they should read the two words one after the other.

Mini-Lesson 1 Compounds

Remind children that...
- Many words are made up of smaller word parts.
- A compound word is made up of two or more shorter words.

Word List

cowboy	sidewalk
pigpen	sunrise
raincoat	uphill

Guide Practice

Use step 3 of the routine above to help children read **compound words**. Remind children that a compound word is a word made up of two or more shorter words. Use letter tiles to form *bathtub* or write the word. Help children identify the two smaller words in *bathtub*. I notice the two parts in this word. Run your hand under *bath*. The first word part is *bath*. Run your hand under *tub*. The second word part is *tub*. To read a compound word, read the two words one after the other: *bath, tub, bathtub.* Continue the same procedure to introduce the remaining words below.

bathtub	goldfish	haircut
highway	popcorn	

If... children have difficulty reading a compound word, **then...** help them identify one part at a time as you cover the remaining part (Routine Card 4).

On Their Own For more practice, use Worktext p. 80 and the Word List. Help children use letter tiles to form and read each word part. Monitor children as they read each word.

 **2 More Compounds**

Remind children that...
- Many words are made up of smaller word parts.
- A compound word is made up of two or more shorter words.
- Many compound words build on a common base word.

Word List

bathroom	anything
bedroom	nothing
homesick	itself
homework	myself

Guide Practice

Remind children that they learned to put two words together to make a compound word. Write *ball* and say it aloud: *ball.* We can add *base* to the beginning of *ball* to make a new word. Write *base* before *ball.* Point to *base* and then to *ball.* Let's read the word parts together: *base, ball, baseball.* Write *ball* again. Many compound words

share a common base word. Write *foot* before *ball.* Point to *foot* and *ball.* Let's read the word parts together to say this word: *foot, ball, football.* Repeat the process with the remaining words. Help children think of other words that share the base words *ball, some,* or *out.*

baseball	football	somebody
something	outfit	outside

If... children cannot read a word,

then... model blending the sounds of each word part and then blend the whole word (Routine Card 2).

On Their Own See Worktext p. 81 and the Word List for additional practice. Ask children to take turns using each word in a sentence. Help children with sound-by-sound blending as needed.

Mini-Lesson 3 Compounds with a Longer Word Part

Remind children that...
- Many words are made up of smaller word parts.
- A compound word is made up of two or more shorter words.
- Some compounds words have a longer word as a word part.

Word List

daydreaming	playground
fingerprint	skyscraper
peppermint	summertime

Guide Practice

Remind children that they learned how to put two words together to make a compound word. Explain that in this lesson they will learn to read compound words that have a longer word as a word part. Write *flower* and *pot.* Say the words with children. You know these words. We can make a compound word by putting a short word (*pot*) together

with a longer word (*flower*). Write *pot* after *flower.* Cover *pot* and read the first word part: *flower.* Then cover *flower* and read *pot*: *pot.* The parts are *flower* and *pot.* Read the word with me: *flower, pot, flowerpot.* Repeat the procedure with the other words below.

flowerpot	firefighter	grasshopper
sunglasses	thunderstorm	

If... children cannot read the words,

then... help them identify the two smaller words and have children read them with you without pausing.

On Their Own For additional practice, use Worktext p. 82 and the Word List. Encourage children to look for compound words as they read.

More Endings and Plurals

Objectives:
- Introduce ending *-es* to words that end in *y.*
- Introduce ending *-ed* to words that end in *y.*
- Introduce irregular plurals.

MATERIALS
- Worktext pp. 83–85
- Routine Cards 1, 2, 4
- Letter tiles

Set the scene Remind children that they have learned different ways to make plural words and have learned to read words that end in *y.* In this lesson, we're going to learn how to add the endings *-es* and *-ed* to words ending in **y.** We will also learn more about making and reading **plurals.**

Routine **1. Connect** Connect the lesson to previous learning. Write *carry* and *cry.* These are words you know. Read them with me: *carry, cry.* Today we will learn how to change these words and others like them into new words by adding the ending *-es.*

2. Model and Give Examples Point to *carry.* When I see a word ending in *y,* I have to change the *y* to an *i* before I can add an *-es* or *-ed* ending. The *i* keeps the sound of the *y* in the word. Say *carry.* Beneath *carry,* write *carry* again. Erase the *y* and insert an *i* in its place. Then add the ending *-es.* Cover the *-es* and read *carry* again. Remind children that you changed the *y* to an *i.* Then point to *-es* and say it aloud: /z/. Say the new word: *carries.*

3. Model Blending Point to the *-es.* When I see a word with *-es* at the end, I figure out the base word. A *y* might have been changed to an *i.* Point to the *i.* Read the base word and then the ending. I read the two parts: *carri, es, carries.* Have children read the word with you. Use it in a sentence: *Juan carries the box.* Repeat the procedure with *cry.*

Mini-Lesson 1 — Ending *-es:* Spelling Change *y* to *i*

Remind children that...
- Word parts can be added to many words to make new words.
- Sometimes adding endings to a word requires a spelling change.
- Before adding *-es* to a word that ends in **y,** the **y** must be changed to an **i.**

Word List
bunnies	ponies
dries	skies
fries	strawberries

Guide Practice
Help children connect *-es* with words ending in **y.** Write *baby.* Beneath it, write *babies.* Have children read both words with you. We can put the word parts *baby* and *-es* together to make the plural word *babies.* Remember that a plural word names more than one. *Baby* is one. *Babies*

is more than one. Point to *i.* We change the *y* in *baby* to an *i* before we add the ending *-es.* Run your hand under *babies.* In this word, the parts are *babi* and *-es.* Read the parts one after the other with me: *babi, es, babies.* Repeat the procedure to introduce the remaining word pairs with the ending *-es.*

baby/babies	city/cities	fly/flies
lady/ladies	story/stories	

If... children have difficulty reading a word, **then...** remind them that the *i* in the new word keeps the sound of the *y* in the base word.

On Their Own Use Worktext p. 83 and the Word List for additional practice. Help children use letter tiles to form and read each word part.

Mini-Lesson 2 — Ending -ed: Spelling Change y to i

Remind children that...
- Word parts can be added to many words to make new words.
- Sometimes adding endings to a word requires a spelling change.
- Before adding *-ed* to a word that ends in *y,* the *y* must be changed to an *i.*

Word List

applied	married
dried	studied
hurried	supplied

Guide Practice

Write *copy* and beneath it, *copies.* Remind children that the *y* at the end of the word (point to *copy*) must be changed to an *i* before an ending can be added. Point to *copies.* Then write *copy* again and beneath it, *copied.* Before you can add *-ed* to a word ending in *y,* change the *y* to an *i.* I say the base word and the ending one after the other to say the word. Have children say the word with you: *copi, ed, copied.* Point to *copied.* The *y* was changed to an *i.* The *i* keeps the same sound as the *y.* Repeat the procedure to introduce the remaining word pairs

copy/copied	fry/fried	reply/replied
try/tried	worry/worried	

If... children cannot read a word,

then... have them identify one part at a time as you cover the remaining parts (Routine Card 4). Model sound-by-sound blending (Routine Card 1) as needed.

On Their Own See Worktext p. 84 and the Word List for additional practice. Help children use each word in a sentence.

Mini-Lesson 3 — Irregular Plurals

Remind children that...
- A plural word names more than one person, place, thing, or idea.
- The plural form of many words is made by adding an ending to its singular form.
- Irregular plurals are very different from their singular forms.

Word List

children	women
geese	teeth
oxen	

Guide Practice

Remind children that they have learned to read plural words that end in *-s* and *-es.* Some plural words look very different from their singular forms. The spelling of these plurals does not follow a pattern. We just have to remember these words. Write *foot.* Then point to and read *foot. Feet* is the plural form of *foot.* Write and say *feet.* The vowels in these words are different. Point to *oo* in *foot* and *ee* in *feet.* Repeat the procedure to help children read the other word pairs below. Remember that some plural words do not end in *-s.*

foot/feet	man/men
mouse/mice	person/people

If... children cannot read a word,

then... use Routine Card 2 to blend the separate sound-spellings. Have children repeat the sounds after you without pausing.

On Their Own For more practice, use Worktext p. 85. For additional practice, help children read the words on the Word List. For each word, write the singular and plural forms next to each other. Have children read each word pair aloud.

Contractions

Objectives:

- Teach concept of contractions.
- Introduce contractions *n't, 'm.*
- Introduce contractions *'s, 'd.*
- Introduce contractions *'re, 've, 'll.*

MATERIALS

- Worktext pp. 86–88
- Routine Card 4

Set the scene Remind children that they learned to read the words *not, am, will, is, had, has, are,* and *have.* Today we will learn to read words by putting words like these together with other words to make **contractions.** Explain that a contraction is a shorter word formed by combining two words. The omitted letters are replaced with an apostrophe.

Routine **1. Connect** To connect today's lesson to previous learning, write *not* and *am.* These are words you know. Let's read them. Today we will learn how to make new words by putting *not* and *am* together with other words you know.

2. Model and Give Examples Write *doesn't. Doesn't* is a contraction. A contraction is a short way of writing two words as one. Beneath *doesn't,* write *does not. Does* and *not* make up the contraction *doesn't. Doesn't* is a short way of writing *does not.* Point to the apostrophe. This punctuation mark is an apostrophe. It takes the place of letters that are left out. Erase the *o* in *not* and insert an apostrophe in its place to make *doesn't.*

3. Model Blending Point to *doesn't* again. When I see a word with an apostrophe, I know it might be a contraction. I notice the two parts in the contraction. In this word, the parts are *does* and *n't.* Ask children to say the parts together to read the word: *does, n't, doesn't.* We learned that an apostrophe can stand for missing letters. What letter does the apostrophe in *doesn't* stand for? Yes, it stands for the *o* in *not.*

Mini-Lesson 1 Contractions *n't, 'm*

Remind children that...

- Word parts can be added to many words to make new words.
- A contraction is a shorter word formed by combining two words.
- In a contraction, the omitted letters are replaced with an apostrophe.
- Many words include the contraction *n't,* and only one word includes the contraction *'m.*

Word List

aren't	isn't
couldn't	haven't
didn't	I'm
hadn't	

Guide Practice

Help children connect *n't* with *not* and *'m* with *am* and combine words. Write *do not* and beneath *do not,* write *don't.* Point to *don't.* We can put the words *do* and *not* together to make the contraction *don't.* Point to the apostrophe. The apostrophe takes the place of the letter *o* in the contraction *don't.* The two parts in *don't* are *do* and *n't.* Have children read the two parts together to read the word: *do, n't, don't.* Repeat the procedure to introduce the word pairs below.

do not/don't	can not/can't
will not/won't	I am/I'm

If... children have difficulty reading a contraction, **then...** use Routine Card 4 to help them identify one word part at a time. Run your hand under the word as they read each part.

On Their Own Use Worktext p. 86 and the Word List for additional practice. Have children identify the two words each contraction stands for.

Mini-Lesson 2 Contractions 's, 'd

Remind children that...
- Word parts can be added to many words to make new words.
- A contraction is a shorter word formed by combining two words.
- In a contraction, the omitted letters are replaced with an apostrophe.
- Many words include the contractions *'s* or *'d.*

Word List

it's	he'd
she's	we'd
what's	you'd

Guide Practice
Write *he's* and beneath *he's,* write *he is. He's* is a contraction. What do you know about reading contractions? When you see a contraction, you know that it is a short way of writing two words. The apostrophe takes the place of the letters that are left out. Erase the *i* in *is* and insert an apostrophe in its place to make *he's.* Notice the two parts in the contraction. Let's read them together to say the word: *he, 's, he's.* Repeat the procedure with the other word pairs below. Explain that, depending on the sentence, *'s* can also stand for the word *has; 'd* can stand for the word *had* or *would.*

he is/he's	**it is/it's**	**she had/she'd**
they had/they'd	**I would/I'd**	

If... children cannot read a contraction,
then... identify the word parts and have children read the parts one after the other with you.

On Their Own See Worktext p. 87 and the Word List for additional practice. Have children use each word in a sentence.

Mini-Lesson 3 Contractions 're, 've, 'll

Remind children that...
- Word parts can be added to many words to make new words.
- A contraction is a shorter word formed by combining two words.
- In a contraction, the omitted letters are replaced with an apostrophe.
- Many words include the contractions *'re, 've,* or *'ll.*

Word List

they're	he'll
I've	I'll
we've	she'll
you've	

Guide Practice
Remind children that they have learned how to make contractions. Today we will learn to connect *'re* with *are,* *'ve* with *have,* and *'ll* with *will* to read more contractions.

Write *we're. We're* is a contraction. Beneath *we're,* write *we are. We* and *are* make up the contraction *we're. We're* is a short way of writing *we are.* Point to the apostrophe. This apostrophe takes the place of letters that are left out. Erase the *a* in *are* and insert an apostrophe in its place to make *we're.* Put the parts together to read the word: *we, 're, we're.* Repeat the procedure to introduce the other contractions below.

we are/we're	**you are/you're**
they have/they've	**you will/you'll**

If... children cannot read a word,
then... read the word parts together as you run your hand beneath them.

On Their Own For more practice, use Worktext p. 88 and form and read the words on the Word List. Have children identify the two words each contraction stands for.

Possessives and Abbreviations

Objectives:
- Teach concepts of possessives and abbreviations.
- Introduce rule for forming possessive form of singular words.
- Introduce rule for forming possessive form of plural words that end in *-s.*
- Introduce common abbreviations.

MATERIALS
- Worktext pp. 89–91
- Routine Cards 1, 2, 4

Set the scene Remind children that they have learned to add endings to make many new words. You have learned to read contractions that contain apostrophes. In this lesson, we will learn to make new words by adding endings with apostrophes and periods.

Routine **1. Connect** Connect today's lesson to previous learning. Write *isn't. Isn't* is a contraction. It is a short way to say *is not.* Read it with me: *is, n't, isn't.* Today we will learn how to make new words that contain apostrophes.

2. Model and Give Examples Write *cat.* Beneath it, write *cat's.* Point to and say each word: *cat, cat's. Cat's* is a possessive. It shows that a person or animal owns or has something. Write *the cat's toy.* Read the words. Circle the *'s* ending. Whose toy is it? It is the cat's toy. The cat owns, or has, the toy. Repeat the process with the name *Sam* and its possessive form, *Sam's.*

3. Model Blending Point to the apostrophe and *s* in *cat's.* The apostrophe and *s* tell me that the toy belongs to one cat. Have children repeat the phrase with you: *the cat's toy.* Add an apostrophe and *s* to a singular word to make it possessive. *The cat's toy* means that the cat has a toy. Remind children that when they see a word with an apostrophe and *s* at the end, they should remember that the word might be a possessive. Tell them they need to think about the meaning of the entire sentence. Then repeat the process above with the name of a child in the group.

Mini-Lesson 1 Singular Possessives

Remind children that…
- A singular word names one person, place, thing, or idea.
- A possessive shows that a person or animal owns or has something.
- Word parts can be added to many words to make new words.
- To make a singular word possessive, add an **apostrophe** and *-s.*

Word List
animal's	girl's
box's	group's
father's	tree's

Guide Practice
Help children make singular words possessive and read singular possessive words. Write *bus* and have children read it: *bus. Bus* is a singular word. It names one thing.

Beneath *bus,* write *bus's.* Point to *bus's. Bus's* is a possessive word. Write *wheels* after *bus's.* Read *bus's wheels* aloud. The **apostrophe** and *s* tell me that the wheels belong to the bus. Circle the apostrophe and *s.* Notice that the apostrophe comes before the *s.* To make a singular word possessive, add an apostrophe and *s.* Repeat the process with the other possessives below. Explain that the *s* sometimes makes the sound /s/ and other times the sound /z/.

boy's   class's   flower's   kid's   pig's

If… children have difficulty reading a word,
then… ask for the sound of each letter or group of letter and then help children blend the words (Routine Card 2).

On Their Own Use Worktext p. 89 and the Word List for additional practice.

 **Plural Possessives**

Remind children that...

- A plural word names more than one person, place, thing, or idea.
- A possessive shows that a person or animal owns or has something.
- Word parts can be added to many words to make new words.
- To make a plural word that ends in *s* possessive, add an **apostrophe.**

Word List

bugs'	kids'	stories'
dresses'	ladies'	teachers'

Guide Practice

Write and say *bird* and *birds.* Remind children of the difference between singular and plural words. Then write *the bird's wings.* Point to *bird's. Bird's* is a singular possessive. The **apostrophe** and *s* show that the wings belong to one bird. Now write *the birds' wings.* Point to *birds'. Birds'* is a plural possessive. Circle the apostrophe. The apostrophe comes after the *s,* so I know that the wings belong to more than one bird. Add just an apostrophe to a plural word that ends in *s* to make it possessive. Repeat the procedure with the other words below.

birds' cities' girls' houses' foxes' mothers'

If... children cannot read a word,

then... point out the *'s* ending (Routine Card 4) and model sound-by-sound blending (Routine Card 1). Help children identify the correct sound for *s'* in each word.

On Their Own See Worktext p. 90 and the Word List for additional practice. Help children use each word in a sentence.

Mini-Lesson 3 Abbreviations

Remind children that...

- An abbreviation is a shortened form of a word.
- Many common abbreviations begin with a capital letter and end with a period.

Word List

Apr.	Mrs.
Feb.	Oct.
Fri.	Nov.
Mon.	

Guide Practice

Write *Mr. Smith* and say it aloud. Point to and spell *Mr.* Explain that an abbreviation is a shortened form of a word. Today we'll learn to read common abbreviations. Write *Mister.* Point to *Mister.* An abbreviation begins with the same capital letter that the whole word begins with. Explain that it ends with a period. All letters in an abbreviation appear in the whole word. Circle the *M* and *r* in Mister. We learn abbreviations by thinking about the whole word and remembering the shortened form. Write the following abbreviations and words. Point to each abbreviation, say it aloud, and have children read it and the word it stands for.

Ave./Avenue	Dr./Doctor	Jan./January
Mon./Monday	St./Street	

If... children cannot read a word,

then... identify the word each abbreviation stands for and then say the word with children.

On Their Own Use Worktext p. 91 for additional practice. For more practice, use the words on the Word List. Help children identify the whole word each abbreviation stands for.

Phonics and Decoding
Student Worktext

Name _____

mop	**sat**	**ten**
ant	**cat**	**pet**
nap	**it**	**fit**

Sam sat here.
We sat with Sam.

Directions Help your child cut out the word cards. Place the cards face down. Then have your child pick a card and identify the first letter of the word and read the word. Help your child use the word in a sentence. Finally, with your child, read aloud the sentences at the bottom.

2 Common Letter-Sound Correspondences

Phonics and Decoding Lesson 1

bat	got	odd
dog	lap	hop
egg	rag	will

The dog got the ball.
Ed will hug the dog.

Directions Help your child cut apart the word cards. Place the cards in a bowl. Take turns with your child picking a card and reading the word. Then have your child identify the first letter of each word and use it in a sentence. Finally, read aloud the sentences at the bottom with your child.

jet	**kid**	**up**
vet	**yes**	**zap**
quit	**ox**	

Ken is a good kid.
Kim got a kiss from Mom.

Directions Help your child cut apart the word cards. Choose a word and ask your child to identify the first letter of the word. Then have your child read the word and use it in a sentence. Finally, with your child, read aloud the sentences at the bottom.

Phonics and Decoding Lesson 1

Name _____

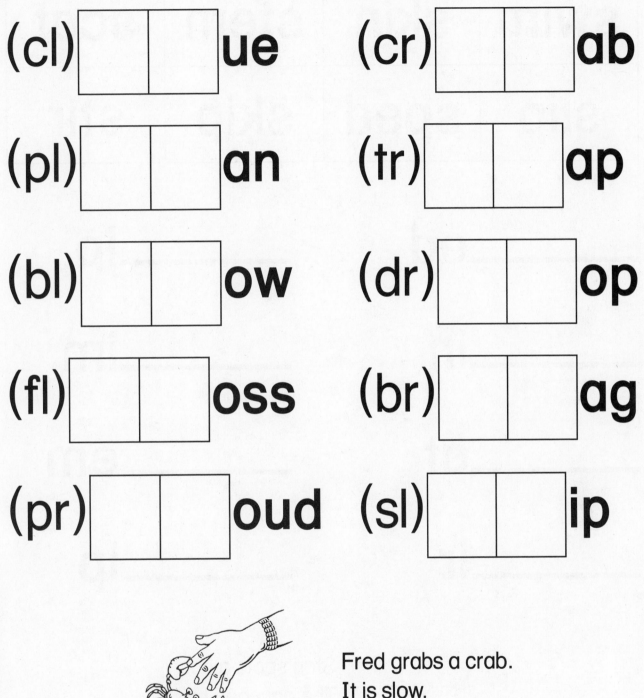

(cl) | | |ue

(cr) | | |ab

(pl) | | |an

(tr) | | |ap

(bl) | | |ow

(dr) | | |op

(fl) | | |oss

(br) | | |ag

(pr) | | |oud

(sl) | | |ip

Fred grabs a crab.
It is slow.

School + Home

Directions Have your child read the blends in parentheses. Then have him or her write those blends in the boxes to make words. Ask your child to say each word aloud and listen for the sounds of the initial blends. Then read aloud the sentences at the bottom and have your child read them aloud after you.

swim	**skin**	**stem**	**scat**
slip	**sped**	**skip**	**stir**

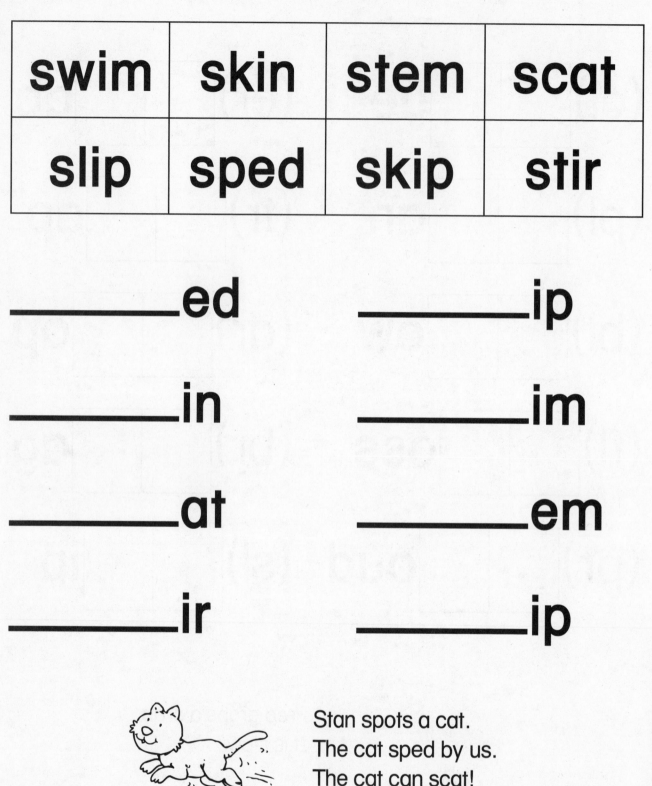

_____ed   _____ip

_____in   _____im

_____at   _____em

_____ir   _____ip

Stan spots a cat.
The cat sped by us.
The cat can scat!

School + Home

Directions Have your child circle the initial **s** blend in each word. Then ask your child to write the words on the lines and say each word aloud, listening for the initial blends. Read the sentences at the bottom and have your child read them after you.

Name _____

scr	spl	spr	squ	str

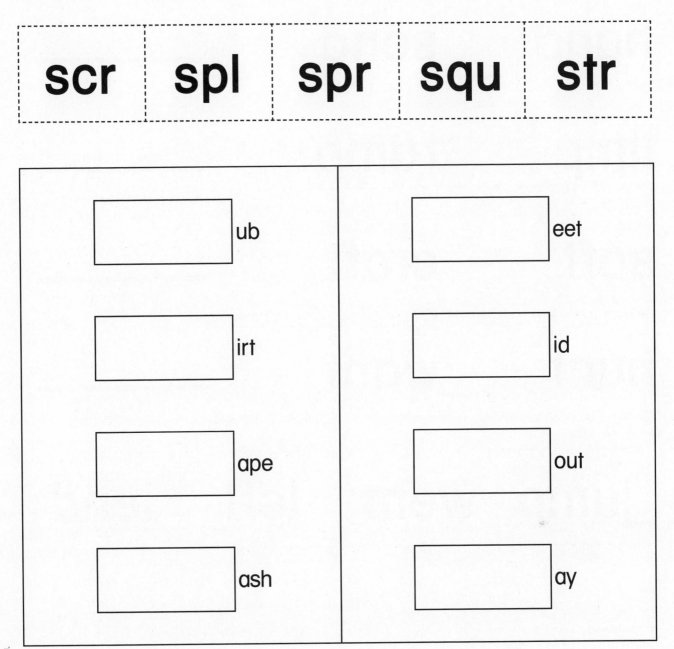

	ub		eet
	irt		id
	ape		out
	ash		ay

The squid sprays the pig.
The pig squirms and squeals.

 **Directions** Have your child cut the cards at the top and use them to build words. Then ask your child to say each word aloud. Read the sentences at the bottom and have your child repeat after you.

hand	send	_____
limp	ramp	_____
soft	craft	_____
hunt	want	_____

jump	went	left	lend

The cat can jump.
Can Kim lend the cat a hand?

Directions Have your child cut apart the four word cards. Ask your child to read aloud the words in the first row. Ask, "Which word card has the same ending sounds as these words?" Then have your child place that card at the end of the row. Repeat with the next three rows. Read the sentences aloud and have your child circle the words with final blends.

School + Home

Phonics and Decoding Lesson 3

Name _____

| lt | ld | lp |

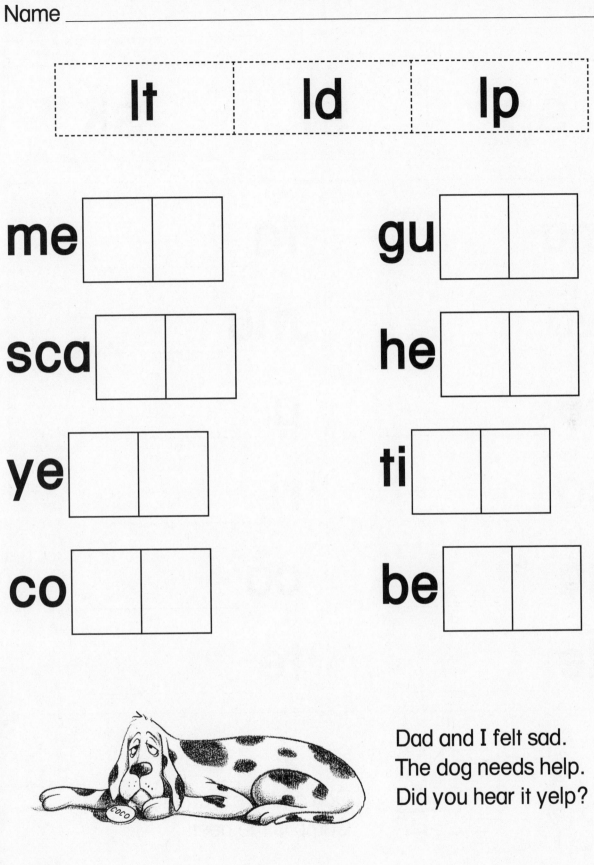

me ☐☐

gu ☐☐

sca ☐☐

he ☐☐

ye ☐☐

ti ☐☐

co ☐☐

be ☐☐

Dad and I felt sad.
The dog needs help.
Did you hear it yelp?

Directions Have your child build words using the final *l* blends at the top of the page. Ask your child to say each word aloud and listen for the final blend. Then read the sentences together. Have your child point to the three words that end in *l* blends.

School + Home

Name _____

sp	st	sk

ma _____	fa _____
wa _____	mu _____
be _____	a _____
co _____	ri _____
ga _____	ca _____
de _____	te _____

Dan and I rest on the grass.
Camp is the best!

School + Home **Directions** Help your child make words by writing one of the final *s* blends on each blank line. Point to each new word and say it aloud with your child, emphasizing the final sound. Then have your child practice reading the sentences at a natural pace.

Phonics and Decoding Lesson 3

she	shot	shark
dish	rash	ship
shut	wish	fish
shoe	shop	bush
cash	shell	short
sheep	dash	share

What dish can she eat?
She can eat fresh fish.

School + Home

Directions Your child learned to read words with the letters *sh.* Help your child read each word aloud. Tell your child to draw a circle around words that begin with *sh* and a box around words that end with *sh.*

Name _____

I like hot [ ][ ][ ][ ][ ] .

(cocoa, baths)

[ ][ ][ ][ ] is fun. (Mark, Math)

Rob is [ ][ ][ ][ ] . (tall, thin)

I [ ][ ][ ][ ][ ] of playing.

(think, dream)

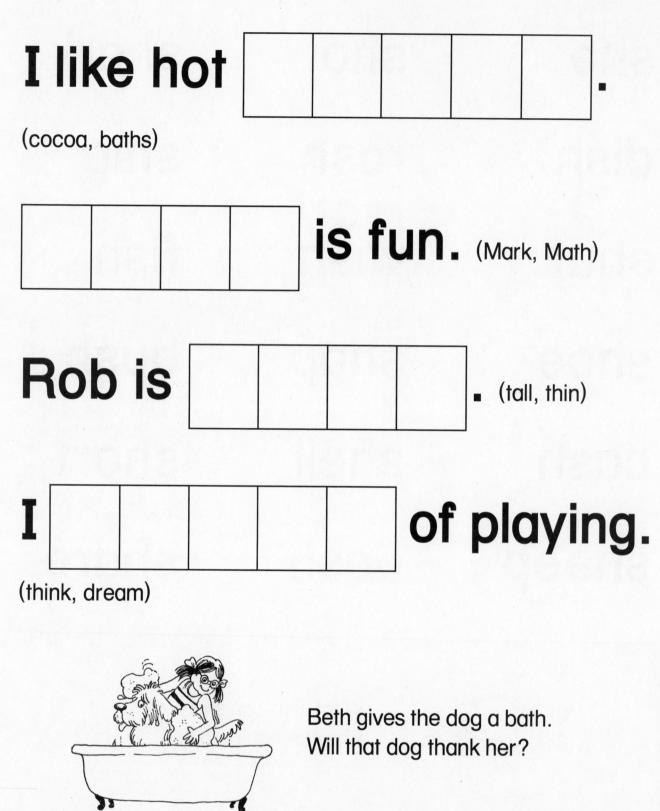

Beth gives the dog a bath.
Will that dog thank her?

Directions Read the first sentence and the words below it. Point to each word as you read. Ask your child which word has the /th/ sound (as in *thought*). Repeat the sentence and the answer choices as needed. Help your child write the word in the boxes. Repeat with each sentence. Then read the sentences at the bottom and have your child circle the words with *th*.

School + Home

12 Consonant Digraphs

Phonics and Decoding Lesson 4

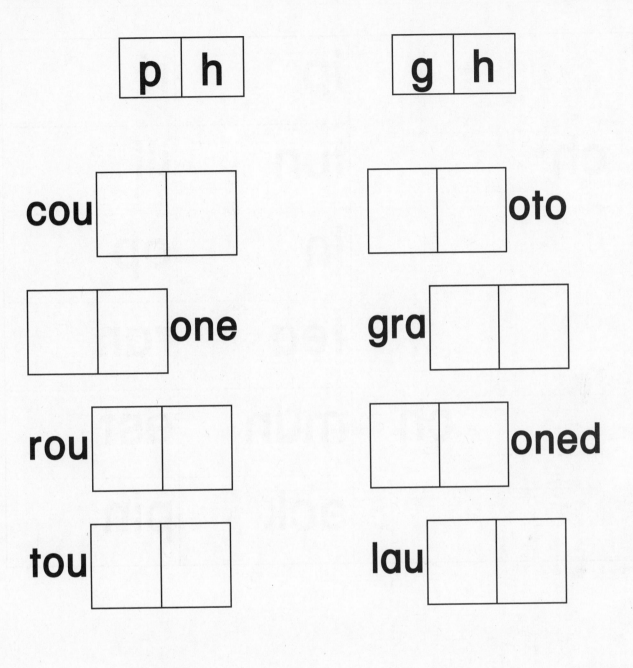

p	h

g	h

cou [ ][ ]

[ ][ ] oto

[ ][ ] one

gra [ ][ ]

rou [ ][ ]

[ ][ ] oned

tou [ ][ ]

lau [ ][ ]

Did you cough?
I will call Phil on the phone.

Directions Help your child make words by choosing *ph* or *gh* to write in the boxes. Point to each word and say it aloud with your child several times. Then read the sentences together. Ask your child to read each sentence aloud as you run your hand under each word.

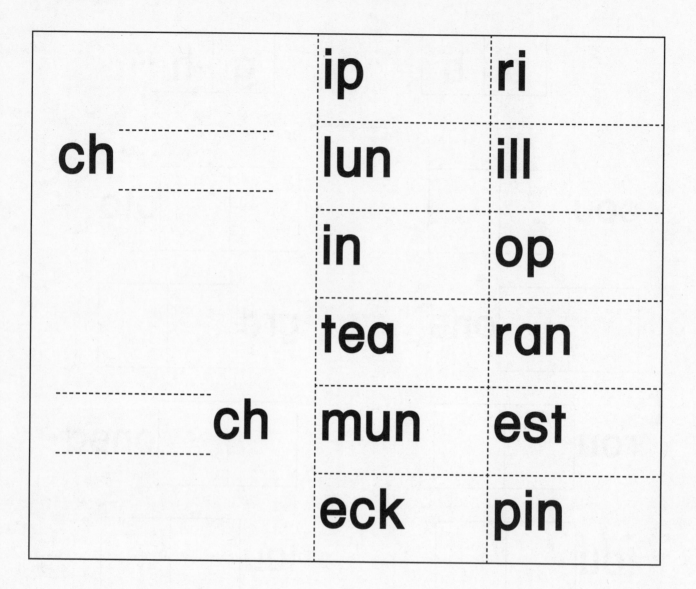

ch _____

ip | ri

lun | ill

in | op

tea | ran

_____ ch mun | est

eck | pin

Ben eats lunch with Chad.
They munch on chips.

Directions Help your child cut apart the letter cards. Have your child pick a card. Ask, "Can you make a word by placing these letters before the *ch* or after the *ch*?" Help your child place the card to build a word and then say the word together. Repeat for each letter card. Then have your child read the sentences aloud.

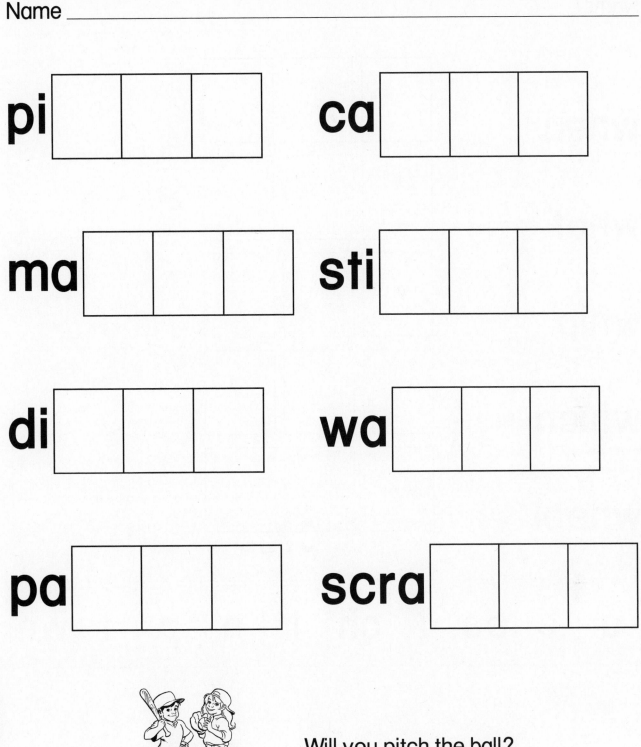

pi ▢ ▢ ▢

ca ▢ ▢ ▢

ma ▢ ▢ ▢

sti ▢ ▢ ▢

di ▢ ▢ ▢

wa ▢ ▢ ▢

pa ▢ ▢ ▢

scra ▢ ▢ ▢

Will you pitch the ball?
Chuck wants to catch it.

Directions Your child learned that the letters *tch* spell the sound /ch/, as in *itch*. Help your child write the letters *t, c,* and *h* in the boxes. Have your child read the words to you. Then read the sentences together and ask your child to point to words that end in /ch/.

Phonics and Decoding Lesson 5

More Consonant Digraphs **15**

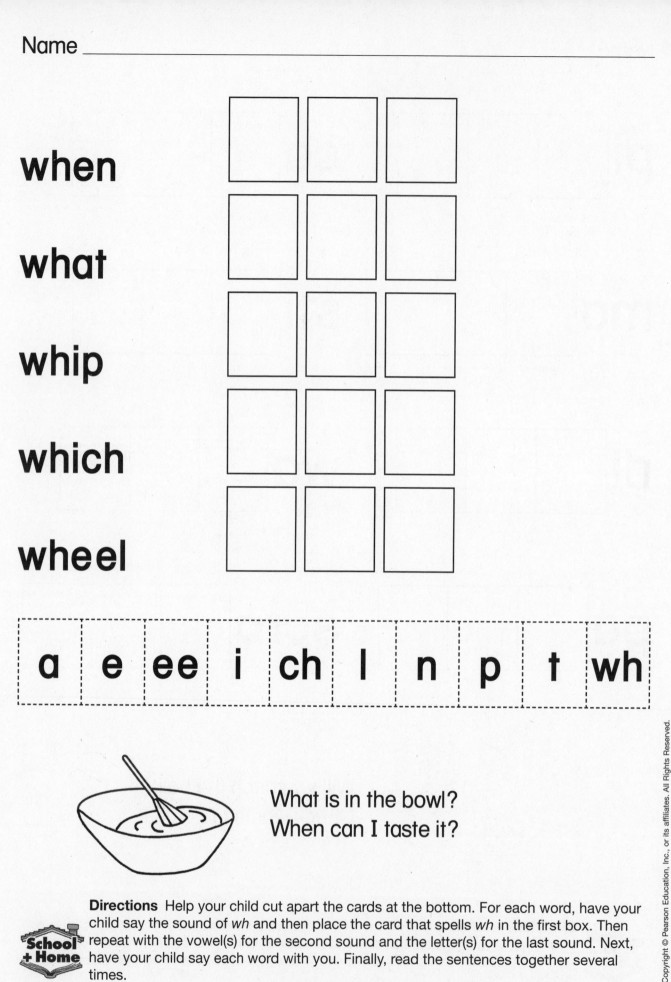

when

what

whip

which

wheel

| a | e | ee | i | ch | l | n | p | t | wh |

What is in the bowl?
When can I taste it?

Directions Help your child cut apart the cards at the bottom. For each word, have your child say the sound of *wh* and then place the card that spells *wh* in the first box. Then repeat with the vowel(s) for the second sound and the letter(s) for the last sound. Next, have your child say each word with you. Finally, read the sentences together several times.

Phonics and Decoding Lesson 5

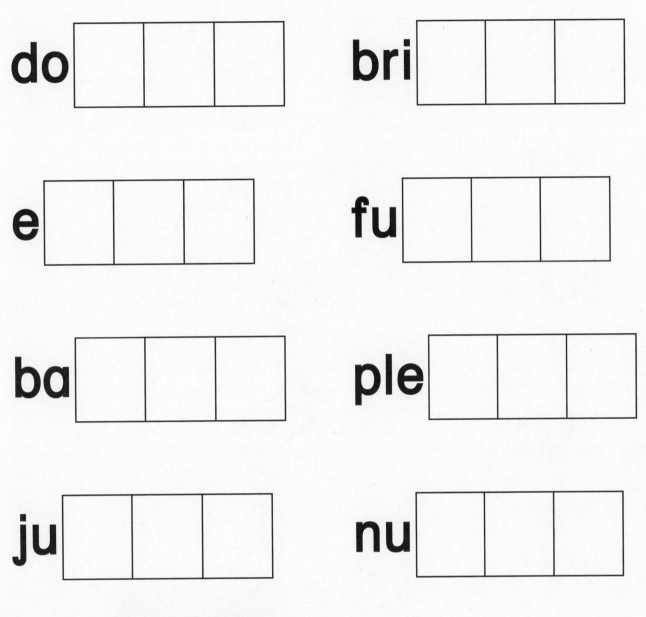

do ☐☐☐

bri ☐☐☐

e ☐☐☐

fu ☐☐☐

ba ☐☐☐

ple ☐☐☐

ju ☐☐☐

nu ☐☐☐

Madge would not budge.
Tim had to nudge her a bit.

Directions Your child learned that the letters *dge* spell the sound /j/, as in *ledge.* Help your child write the letters *d, g,* and *e* in the boxes. Then read the words and the sentences below together.

School + Home

sink

ring

link

bank

drink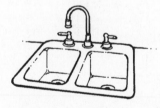

Hank can wink.
His pal Frank can only blink.

Copyright © Pearson Education, Inc., or its affiliates. All Rights Reserved.

School + Home **Directions** Have your child read aloud each word and draw a line to the matching picture. Then read the sentences together.

Name _____

I saw a _____ rock.

(black, big)

Did you _____ the car?

(see, lock)

That was _____.

(fun, quick)

I _____ the ball hard.

(kick, throw)

Nick is sick.
Rick sat on the deck.

Directions Read the first sentence and the answer choices in parentheses. Point to each word as you read. Ask your child which answer choice has the /k/ sound. Help your child write that word on the line. Repeat with each sentence. Then read the sentences about the boys and have your child circle the words with *ck*.

Name _____

am

h

j

sl

ank

b

t

dr

ack

s

bl

ag

fl

r

Jack packs a sack.
The bag has a snack for Frank.
Did Jack eat ham with jam?

School + Home

Directions Help your child write letters in the boxes to build words that end with -am, -ank, -ack, and -ag. Have your child say each word aloud. Then read the sentences together. Ask your child to point to each word that ends with a pattern with short a.

| spill | chop | trick | rock | shop | lock |
| kick | drop | will | stop | sock | drill |

-ill	-ick	-ock	-op

Jill stops to put on socks.
She is quick.
Will Jill do tricks?

Directions Help your child cut out the word cards. Pick one card and read it aloud. Point to the word parts *-ill, -ick, -ock,* and *op* in the chart. Ask, "Which word part is at the end of this word?" Have your child place the card in the appropriate column. Repeat with each word card. Then have your child tell you other words that could fit in each column. Finally, read the words and the sentences with your child.

Phonics and Decoding Lesson 7

Short Vowel Phonograms **21**

Word Bank

bell	nest	yell	drum	bed	trunk
gum	plum	test	sled	plug	skunk

That red trunk is the best!
It is full of junk.
The bugs hum around it.

Directions Read each word in the Word Bank with your child. Then point to the first word and ask your child if it matches one of the pictures. If it does, have your child write the word in the boxes in the same row as the picture. If it does not match a picture, move to the next word. Repeat until your child has identified and written the word that matches each picture. Then help your child read the sentences with you.

Name _____

-ace   -ice

(l) ▢ ace   (m) ▢ ice

(r) ▢ ace   (r) ▢ ice

(sp) ▢▢ ace   (sp) ▢▢ ice

(pl) ▢▢ ace   (n) ▢ ice

Who will win the race?
Bruce has the fastest pace.
Look at his face!

School + Home

Directions Read aloud *-ace* and *-ice.* Then have your child write the initial letters on the left for each word. Say each word several times with your child. Then help your child read the sentences.

Name _____

I am a home for a pet bird.
(cage, large)

I am an animal with a long neck.
(stage, giraffe)

I am a word for *very big.*
(change, huge)

I am something that can make you sick.
(germ, strange)

I am a person or thing of large size.
(age, giant)

Gene saw a large giraffe.
It had a strange tail and huge ears.

School + Home

Directions Read each riddle and the two answer choices with your child. Then ask your child to decide which answer choice is correct. Have your child draw a circle around the correct word. Finally, read the sentences at the bottom together. Have your child draw a circle around each word that has the sound /j/ spelled *g.*

his	nose	tells
these	use	is
wise	dogs	was

Jack has a hose.
He uses it to water his rose.
His rose is red.

Directions Help your child cut apart the word cards. Then turn the word cards face down. Take turns picking a card and reading the word. Help your child use each word in a sentence. Finally, read the sentences at the bottom together.

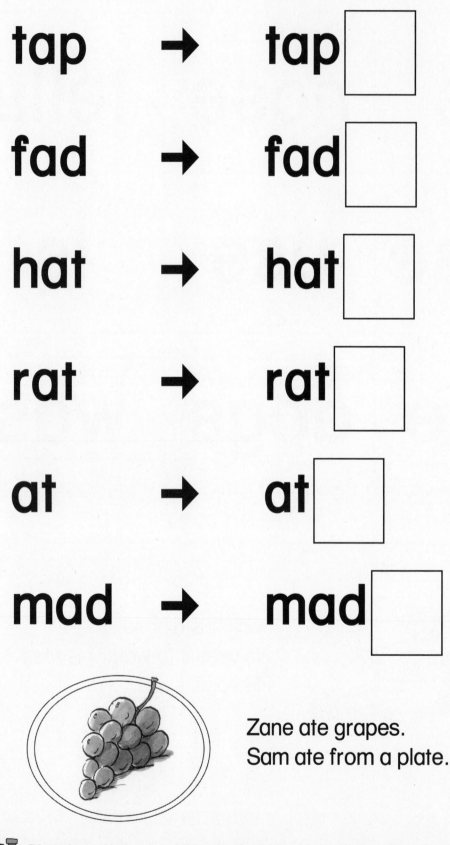

tap → tap ☐

fad → fad ☐

hat → hat ☐

rat → rat ☐

at → at ☐

mad → mad ☐

Zane ate grapes.
Sam ate from a plate.

Directions Help your child write the letter *e* in each box. Then have your child read each pair of words. Encourage your child to make up a sentence using one pair of words. Finally, help your child read the sentences at the bottom.

Word Bank

hike	dive	ride	fine	ripe	side
kite	hide	size	wide	nice	dime

hid → ☐☐☐☐

fin → ☐☐☐☐

kit → ☐☐☐☐

dim → ☐☐☐☐

rip → ☐☐☐☐

Rise and shine!
It is a nice time to wake up.

Directions Read each word in the Word Bank. Then point to the word *hid* below the Word Bank. Help your child write those letters in the first three boxes. Then have your child write *e* in the last box. Say the word together and have your child circle the matching word in the Word Bank. Repeat for each row. Finally, read the sentences together.

School + Home

rob   robe

mop   mope

rod   rode

not   note

hop   hope

Cole rode in the car.
He was close to home.

School + Home

Directions Help your child read the two words in the first row aloud. Ask your child to draw a circle around the word that matches the picture. Repeat for the other rows. Then read the sentences with your child.

Phonics and Decoding Lesson 9

Name _____

Word Bank

tune	cute	June	rule
mule	Zeke	flute	Eve

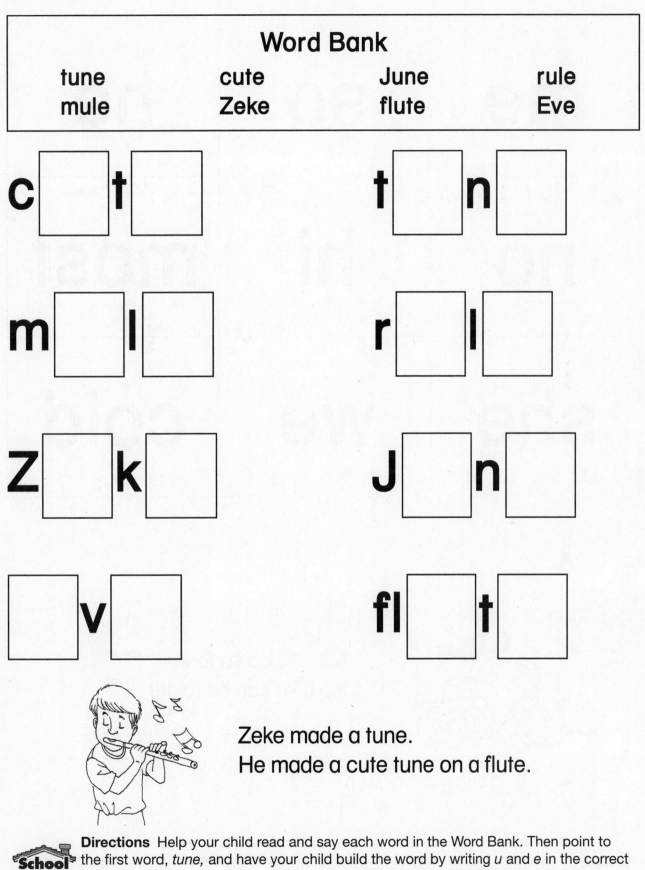

c ☐ t ☐

t ☐ n ☐

m ☐ l ☐

r ☐ l ☐

Z ☐ k ☐

J ☐ n ☐

☐ v ☐

fl ☐ t ☐

Zeke made a tune.
He made a cute tune on a flute.

Directions Help your child read and say each word in the Word Bank. Then point to the first word, *tune,* and have your child build the word by writing *u* and *e* in the correct boxes. Continue with each word in the Word Bank. Then read the sentences aloud together.

Phonics and Decoding Lesson 10

Other Long Vowel Patterns **29**

me	so	he
no	hi	most
she	we	cold

Mo can go so fast.
No bike can be faster.

Directions Have your child read and say each word. Then help your child cut apart the word cards. Turn the word cards face down. Take turns picking a card and reading the word. Help your child use each word in a sentence. Then read the sentences at the bottom together.

School + Home

Phonics and Decoding Lesson 10

I like to ride _____ bike. (his, my)

_____ are you so late? (Why, When)

The _____ drives a bus. (man, lady)

That joke was _____.

(funny, good)

Why did the lady pick up the baby?
She did not want the baby to cry.
The baby is happy!

Directions Read each sentence to your child. Help your child read the words in parentheses aloud. Have your child circle the word in parentheses that has the long *i* sound as in *cry*. Then run your hand under each word as you read all the sentences to your child.

sips	fixes	picks
passes	hops	waxes
packs	misses	tags
digs	kisses	yells
locks	rugs	mixes

Jim passes the can to Kim.
Kim hits it.
Jim nods and hums.

Directions Help your child cut apart the word cards. Spread them out on a table. Have your child sort the cards into two piles: words that end in *-s* and words that end in *-es*. Have your child read each word as he or she places the card into the correct pile. Finally, read the sentences together.

School + Home

Phonics and Decoding Lesson 11

pick ▢▢

mix ▢▢

kiss ▢▢

spill ▢▢

buzz ▢▢

pack ▢▢

fill ▢▢

miss ▢▢

yell ▢▢

spell ▢▢

Pat picked a box.
Pat filled it with rocks.

Directions Have your child say each word as you point to it. Have your child write *ed* in the boxes to build a new word. Practice saying each new word together. Finally, help your child read the sentences.

Name _____

Word Bank

passing	fixing	adding	buzzing	licking
hissing	selling	passing	missing	mixing

The dogs are passing the cats.
The cats are hissing.

School + Home

Directions Read the Word Bank and with your child. Help your child pick the four words that match the pictures. Have your child write the correct words in the boxes. Then read the sentences together.

34 Endings

Phonics and Decoding Lesson 11

kitten

picnic

bottom

basket

rabbit

rab	nic	bot	ket	tom
kit	bas	bit	pic	ten

Where are the kittens?
They are in the bottom
of the picnic basket.

Directions Read each word together. Then help your child cut apart the syllable cards. Have your child build each word using the syllable cards. Place them next to the matching word in the left column. Have your child read each word with you. Finally, help your child read the sentences aloud.

pilot	silent	robot
open	broken	student
music	silent	behind
bonus	open	pilot
broken	music	behind
student	robot	bonus

When will the music begin?
The crowd is silent.

Directions Help your child cut apart the word cards. Arrange them in rows face down. Take turns picking up two cards. Read each word. If the words match, keep the cards. If they do not match, put them back on the table. Continue until all cards have been matched. Then read the sentences with your child.

Phonics and Decoding Lesson 12

Name _____

I saw a <u>camel</u>.

Did you swim in the <u>river</u>?

There are <u>seven</u> girls on my team.

I will <u>finish</u> the book.

The <u>lemon</u> fell from a tree.

I have never seen a camel.
I may visit the camel in the zoo soon.

Directions Help your child read each sentence. Ask your child to draw a line between the two syllables in each underlined word. Then read the sentences about the camel with your child.

Syllable Patterns **37**

Name _____

Dad drives the ☐☐☐ . (van, car)

I like the ☐☐☐☐ . (show, park)

Where is ☐☐☐☐ ? (Mark, Anna)

Pat is ☐☐☐☐ . (funny, smart)

Dogs can ☐☐☐☐ . (bark, heel)

The hens are in the barn on the farm.
The barn is by my yard.

 Directions Read each sentence to your child and the answer choices in parentheses. Try both answer choices in the blank. Have your child circle the word that has the /ar/ sound as in *farm*. Then point to each word as you read all the sentences to your child.

store	oar	snore
short	torn	storm
north	fort	more
roar	fork	before

The pig snorts and snores.
What a chore to give him
more food.

Directions Read each word with your child. Then help your child cut apart the word cards. Mix them up. Have your child sort the cards into three groups: words spelled *or*, words spelled *ore*, and words spelled *oar*. Finally, read the sentences. Ask your child which of the three groups the words *snorts* and *chore* belong in.

Name _____

Word Bank

turn	dirt	girl	burn
first	herd	bird	germ

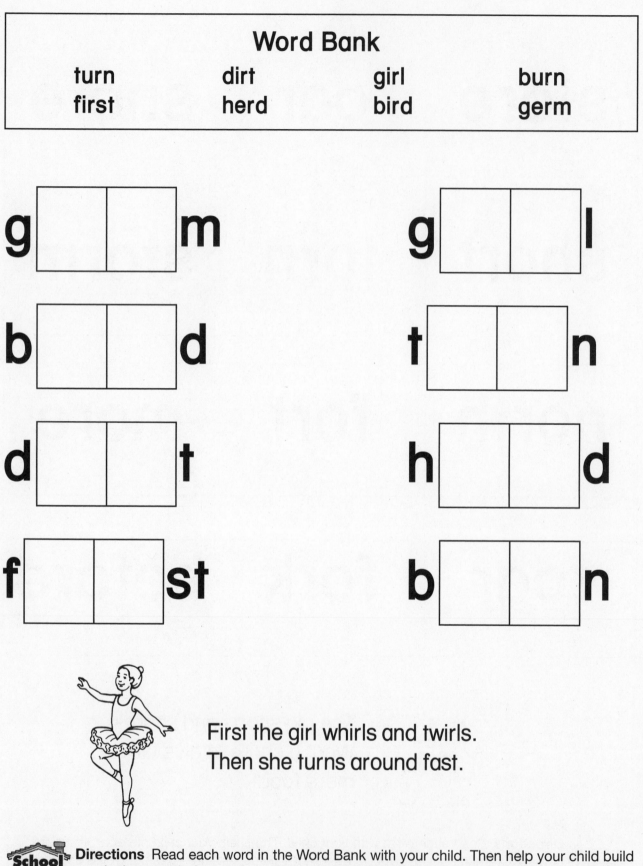

g ☐|☐ m   g ☐|☐ l

b ☐|☐ d   t ☐|☐ n

d ☐|☐ t   h ☐|☐ d

f ☐|☐ st   b ☐|☐ n

First the girl whirls and twirls.
Then she turns around fast.

Directions Read each word in the Word Bank with your child. Then help your child build words that match the words in the Word Bank by writing *er, ir,* or *ur* in the boxes. Read the sentences to your child as you point to each word.

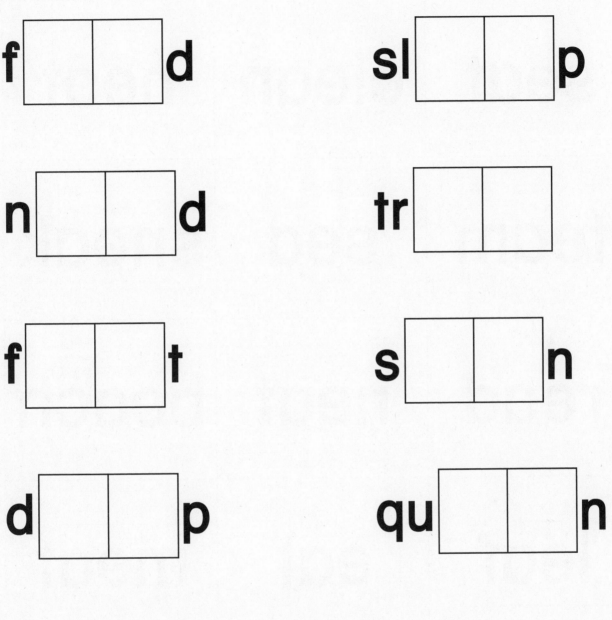

f ☐☐ **d**

sl ☐☐ **p**

n ☐☐ **d**

tr ☐☐

f ☐☐ **t**

s ☐☐ **n**

d ☐☐ **p**

qu ☐☐ **n**

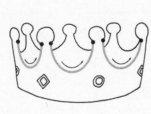

We want to see the queen.
Do we need to kneel?

Directions Your child learned that the long *e* sound can be spelled with *ee*. Help your child build words by writing *ee* in the boxes. Say the new word together. Then ask your child to point to each word as you read the sentences. Have your child circle words in the sentences that are spelled with *ee*.

Phonics and Decoding Lesson 14

Vowel Digraphs (Long e *and* a) **41**

seat	clean	heat
team	sea	sneak
read	neat	beach
leaf	eat	meat

Please take a seat.
Dean has a meal to eat.

Directions Help your child cut out the word cards and place them face up. Say a word and have your child pick up the matching word card. Continue until your child has picked up all the cards. Then point to each word as you read the sentences aloud.

main	day	play
tail	pain	train
stay	wait	mail
brain	clay	say

Gail likes to play with clay.
May she play with it today?

Directions Your child learned that the long *a* sound can be spelled with *ai* or *ay*. Help your child cut out the word cards. Then have your child sort the word cards into two piles: words with *ai* and words with *ay*. Say each word with your child. Run your hand under each word as you read the sentences aloud.

crow	blow	know
row	slow	below
show	mow	window
throw	flow	snow

Look below the window.
Did the wind blow the snow?

School + Home

Directions Say a word and have your child point to the matching word. Have your child say it aloud and then use the word in a sentence. Then read the sentences at the bottom with your child and have him or her point to each word with the letters *ow*.

44 Vowel Digraphs (Long *o* and *i*)

Phonics and Decoding Lesson 15

Name _____

Word Bank

float	foam	coach	goat
road	soap	load	soak

1. f __ __ m

2. g __ __ t

3. l __ __ d

4. s __ __ p

5. s __ __ k

6. fl __ __ t

I want to soak in the water.
Why does the soap float?

Directions Read each word in the Word Bank together. For each numbered item, have your child write the letters *oa* on the lines to build a word. Have your child check his or her completed word by finding a match for it in the Word Bank. Say each completed word together. Finally, have your child read the sentences.

tie

night

dies

right

sigh

lie

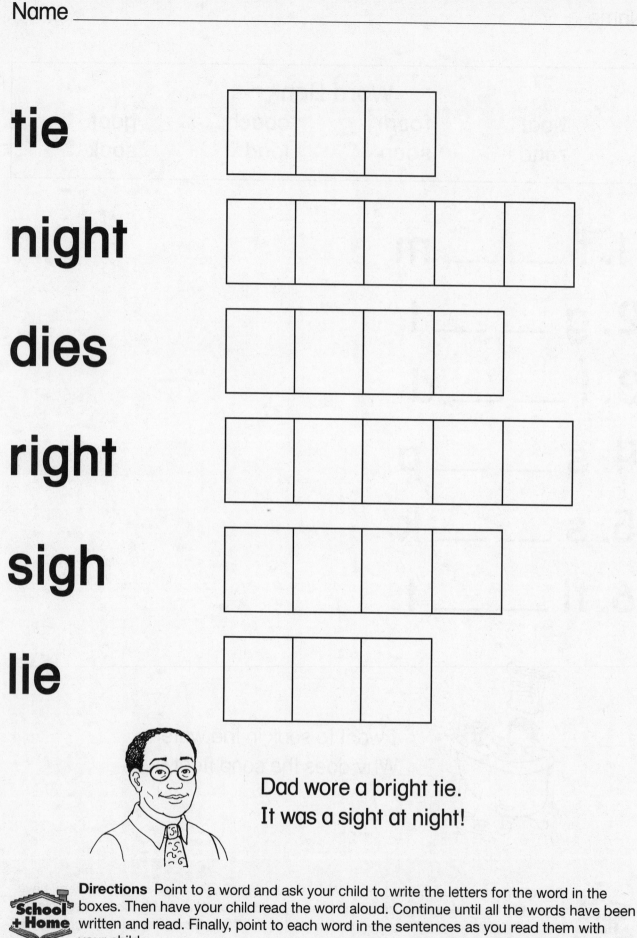

Dad wore a bright tie.
It was a sight at night!

Directions Point to a word and ask your child to write the letters for the word in the boxes. Then have your child read the word aloud. Continue until all the words have been written and read. Finally, point to each word in the sentences as you read them with your child.

Name _____

head	**breath**	**ready**
sweat	**heavy**	**bread**

The big bag is _____.	We got a loaf of _____.
This hat fits my _____.	Are you _____ to go?
Take a deep _____.	I _____ when it is hot.

The bread is very fresh!
I will spread jelly on the bread.

Directions Help your child cut apart the sentence and word cards. Keep them in separate groups and place them face up. Then point to and read a sentence card. Have your child pick the word card that completes the sentence and place it above the blank line. Continue until all the sentences are complete. Have your child point to each word as you read the sentences at the bottom.

Word Bank

book	stood	shook	hood
good	look	cook	

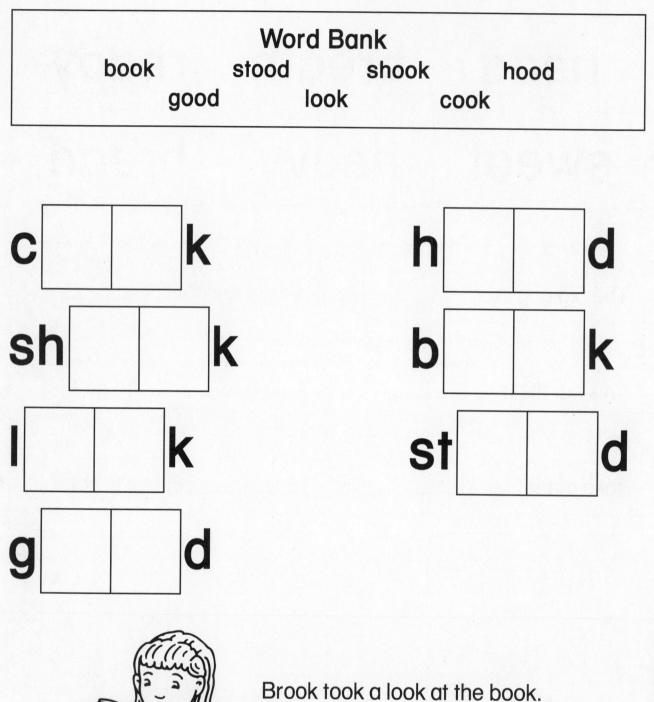

c [ ] [ ] k   h [ ] [ ] d

sh [ ] [ ] k   b [ ] [ ] k

l [ ] [ ] k   st [ ] [ ] d

g [ ] [ ] d

Brook took a look at the book.
She wants to be a good cook.

Directions Have your child read each word in the Word Bank. Ask your child to build words by writing *oo* in the boxes. Help your child check that the word he or she has built matches a word in the Word Bank. Say the word together. Finally, ask your child to read the sentences as you point to each word.

School + Home

Name _____

piece	key	field
honey	monkey	chief
field	piece	honey
chief	monkey	key

Tom had a piece of turkey.
I had some bread with honey.

Directions Have your child cut apart the word cards and place them face down. Take turns picking up two cards. Say each word. If the words match, keep them. If they do not match, place them back on the table. Continue the game until all the words have been picked up. Finally, have your child read the sentences as you point to each word.

1. We clean with a br ___ m.

2. A hammer is a t ___ l.

3. Stan was in a bad m ___ d.

4. Is the z ___ open?

5. I will go to my r ___ m.

At noon the pooch went to the zoo.
He jumped into the pool to get cool.

Directions Help your child read each sentence. Ask him or her to write the letters *oo* on the line to build a word. Say the new word with your child. Then help your child read the sentence again as you point to each word. Finally, read the sentences at the bottom with your child.

School + Home

Name _____

1. Our plants _____.

(grew, died)

2. Dad made beef _____.

(patties, stew)

3. The bird _____.

(sang, flew)

4. The wind _____.

(blew, came)

5. The ship has a big _____.

(sail, crew)

Geese flew across the sky.
Then a leaf blew past me.

Directions Help your child read the first sentence and the two words below it. Have your child circle the word that contains the /ü/ sound as in *drew*. Repeat with the other sentences. Finally, read all the sentences together.

blue	fruit	glue
bruise	true	juice

ue

ui

1. _____   _____

2. _____   _____

3. _____   _____

What is that fruit?
Here is a clue.
It is not blue.

Directions Have your child cut apart the word cards. Place them face down. Ask your child to pick a card and read it. Then have your child look at the word's spelling and decide whether to place it in the *ue* or the *ui* list. Finally, have your child read the sentences as you point to each word.

School + Home

cloud	round	shout
mouse	sound	proud
mouth	house	loud
about	out	found

The hound made a loud sound.
He found a mouse on the ground.

Directions Help your child read each word and cut apart the word cards. Ask your child to select a card and say it aloud. Work together to use each word in a sentence. Finally, read the sentences aloud, pointing to each word as you read.

Name _____

cow

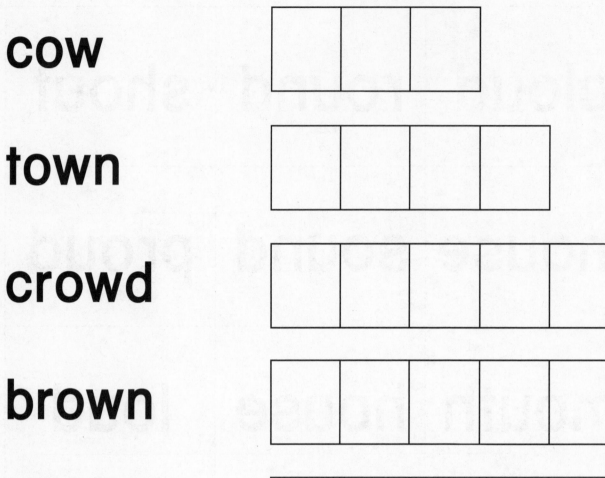

town

crowd

brown

clown

Now the clown has brown shoes.
How did the crowd like the clown?

School + Home

Directions Point to each word and read it together. Have your child write the letters for the word in the boxes. Then ask your child to read the word aloud. Continue until all the words have been written and read. Point to each word as you read the sentences with your child.

enjoy	spoil	point
toy	voice	joy

boil	boy
_____	_____
_____	_____
_____	_____
_____	_____
_____	_____

Troy found some coins in the soil.
He will enjoy his new toy.

Directions Help your child cut apart the word cards. Pick a word and have your child read it aloud. Then have your child place the card under the word in the chart with either the *oi* or the *oy* spelling. When all the cards are on the chart, have your child remove one card at a time and write the word on the line. Read the sentences with your child.

Name _____

Word Bank

halt	small	salt
walk	fall	chalk

1. h __ _____

2. w __ _____

3. sm __ _____

4. s __ _____

5. ch __ _____

6. f __ _____

Walt will walk to the mall.
He will get a small ball and some chalk.

Directions Read the Word Bank with your child. For each numbered word, have your child decide what letters are needed to complete the word. Then have your child write and say the completed word on the line. Check that the word matches a word in the Word Bank. Then, with your child, read the sentences as you point to each word.

School + Home

launch	**paw**	**draw**
crawl	**fault**	**cause**
yawn	**haunt**	**hawk**
pause	**dawn**	**sauce**

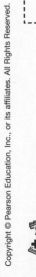

Paul saw a hawk last August.
Why did it pause on a branch?
Then it flew across the lawn.

Directions Help your child cut apart the word cards. Place them face up. Then say a word and have your child point to the matching word card and say the word aloud. Read the sentences together. Have your child circle the letters *au* or *aw* that stand for the sound /ȯ/.

1. bought   boat   barn

2. then   throw   thought

3. corn   caught   clown

4. fought   food   feed

5. train   taught   towel

6. bowl   broom   brought

Joan thought she bought a smart puppy. She brought it home and taught it tricks.

Copyright © Pearson Education, Inc., or its affiliates. All Rights Reserved.

School + Home **Directions** Help your child read each row of words. Have your child circle the word that has the /ȯ/ sound as in *taught*. Then have your child read the sentences aloud.

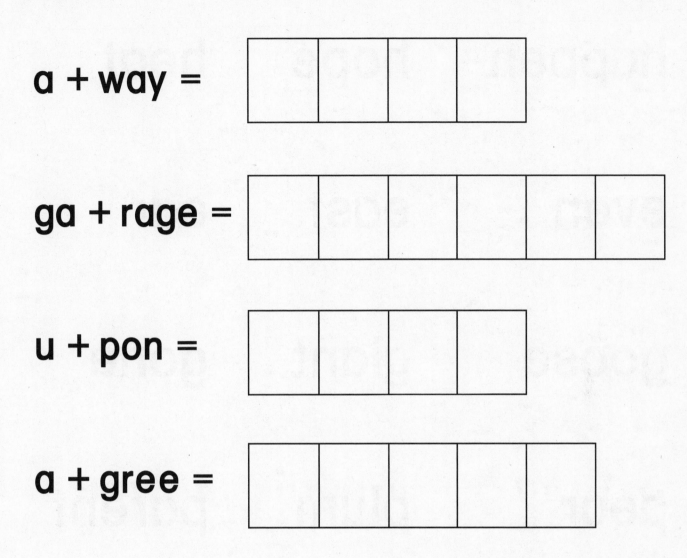

a + way =

ga + rage =

u + pon =

a + gree =

Amanda needs to put away her things. Do you agree?

School + Home

Directions Point to the parts of the first word and say them aloud with your child. Have your child build the whole word by writing the letters in the boxes on the right. Ask your child to read the whole word aloud. Repeat with the other words. Then read the sentences together.

happen	hope	heat
even	east	ear
goose	giant	gone
pear	plum	parent

The children look the same.
They happen to be twins!

Directions Read each row of words. Have your child circle the word that has the schwa sound in the second syllable (*happen, even, giant,* and *parent*).

Phonics and Decoding Lesson 20

Word Bank

gone	sign	dust	gnome	whistle
mist	gum	fasten	listen	nest

1. _____

2. _____

3. _____

4. _____

5. _____

The friends pointed to the "fasten your seatbelt" sign.
They will listen and buckle up.

Directions Read each word in the Word Bank to your child. Have your child circle the words that have silent letters (/n/ spelled *gn*: *gnome, sign*; /s/ spelled *st*: *fasten, listen, whistle*). Then have your child write the words on the lines. Finally, read the sentences together.

knot	knock	knee
knob	knife	

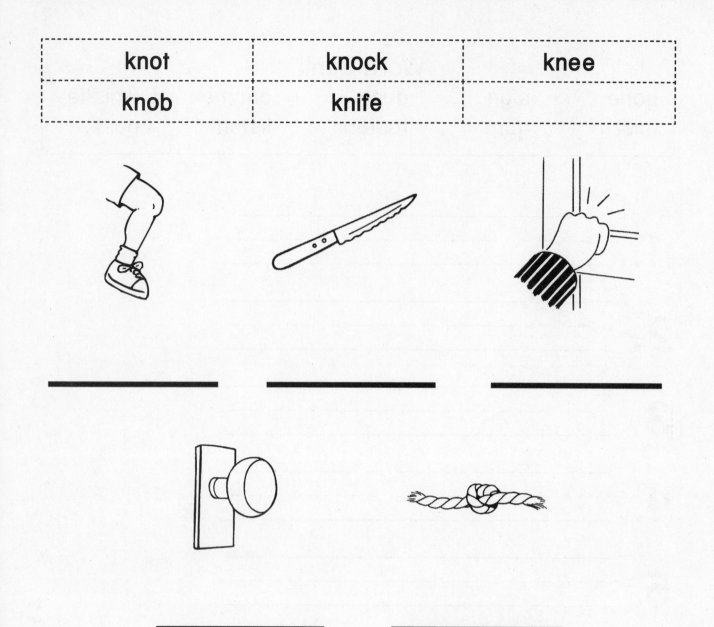

_____   _____   _____

_____   _____

A knight knocked on the door.
He knew the knob was stuck.

Directions Help your child cut out the word cards. Select a word card and have your child read the word with you. Then have him or her place the card below the picture it matches. Repeat with each card. Ask your child to point to each word that begins with *kn* as you read the sentences aloud.

    Phonics and Decoding Lesson 21

wing	**write**	**west**
wrote	**wrist**	**writing**
wreck	**white**	**wheel**

I wrote a story.
It tells how I broke my wrist.
Can you read my writing?

Directions Help your child cut out the word cards. Have your child read the words and separate them into two groups: words with the /r/ sound, as in *write*, and words with no /r/ sound. Then read the sentences.

limb	(sheep)	thumb
(bread slice)	climb	(comb)
lamb	(branch)	crumb
(child climbing tree)	comb	(thumb)

Rose climbed an icy limb.
Her thumbs felt numb.

School + Home

Directions Help your child cut out the word and picture cards. Place them face up. Then take turns reading a word and selecting the matching picture card. Then ask your child to cross out the letter that is silent (*b*). Finally, read the sentences aloud and have your child point to each word as you read.

Phonics and Decoding Lesson 21

Name _____

| b | l | e | | d | l | e | | p | l | e |

ta [ ][ ][ ]   sim [ ][ ][ ]

han [ ][ ][ ]   tum [ ][ ][ ]

bun [ ][ ][ ]   peb [ ][ ][ ]

pud [ ][ ][ ]   sam [ ][ ][ ]

ap [ ][ ][ ]   fid [ ][ ][ ]

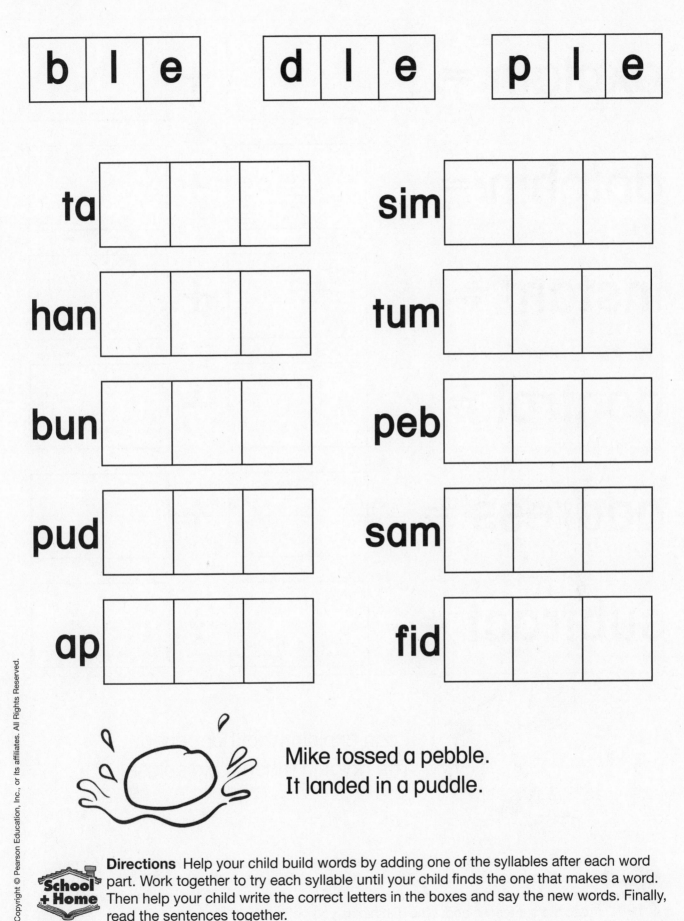

Mike tossed a pebble.
It landed in a puddle.

Directions Help your child build words by adding one of the syllables after each word part. Work together to try each syllable until your child finds the one that makes a word. Then help your child write the correct letters in the boxes and say the new words. Finally, read the sentences together.

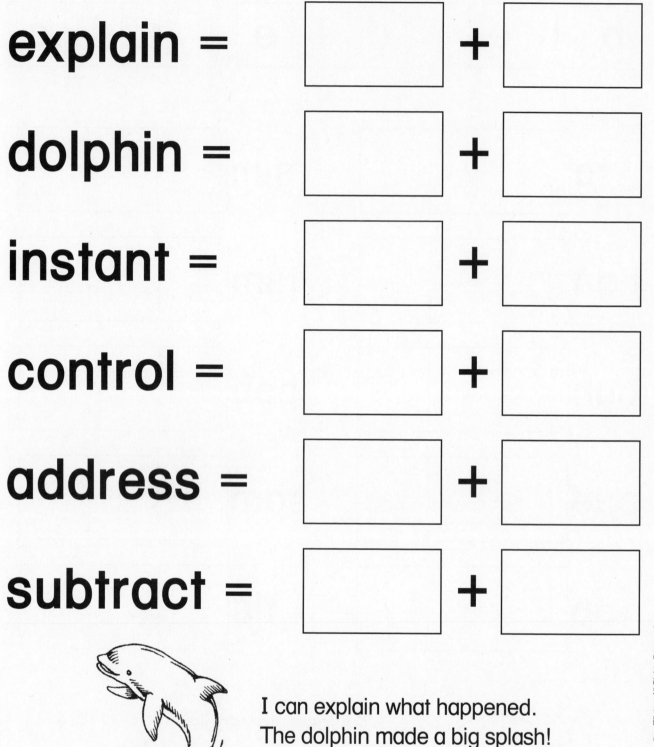

explain = ☐ + ☐

dolphin = ☐ + ☐

instant = ☐ + ☐

control = ☐ + ☐

address = ☐ + ☐

subtract = ☐ + ☐

I can explain what happened.
The dolphin made a big splash!

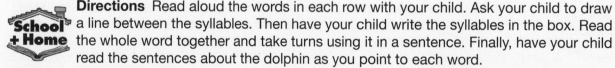

Directions Read aloud the words in each row with your child. Ask your child to draw a line between the syllables. Then have your child write the syllables in the box. Read the whole word together and take turns using it in a sentence. Finally, have your child read the sentences about the dolphin as you point to each word.

Phonics and Decoding Lesson 22

li	in	ru	em	ow
me	ant	on	gi	po

poem

lion

meow

ruin

giant

Noah wrote a silly poem.
It's about a quiet lion that won't roar.
What a funny poet!

Directions First, help your child cut apart the syllable cards. For each word, have your child draw a line between the two vowels. Ask your child to find the two syllable cards needed to make the word. Help your child place the cards in the right order in the boxes next to the word. Repeat with each word. Then read each word and the sentences at the bottom with your child.

Name _____

She will _____ the story.

(read, reread)

Do you _____ glass jars?

(recycle, have)

Mike looked sick and _____.

(sad, unhappy)

The movers will _____ the truck later.

(park, unload)

Please _____ my glass with water.

(bring, refill)

Mom can unwrap her gift now.
Will she recycle the paper?

Directions Help your child read the first sentence and the two words in parentheses below. Ask your child which word has the prefix *re-* or *un-*. Have your child circle the correct word. Repeat with each sentence. Then read the sentences at the bottom with your child.

actor	player	teacher
reader	sailor	inventor
seller	worker	collector
counter	visitor	reporter

The visitor looked into the room.
She was a reporter.
She spoke to our teacher.

Directions Help your child cut apart the word cards. Spread them out on a table. Have your child sort the cards into two piles: words that end in *-er* and words that end in *-or*. Have your child read each word as he or she places the card into the correct pile. Finally, read the sentences together.

Name _____

ful	ly

peace_____ spoon_____

smooth_____ hope_____

glad_____ cup_____

pain_____ main_____

tight_____ fear_____

The cook was careful.
She held the spoon tightly.
She added a cupful of milk.

Directions Point to the two suffixes in the box. Have your child read them and then read each word below. Tell your child to decide how to build a new word by adding one of the two suffixes on the line after each word. After your child has written the suffix on the line, read the word aloud together. Take turns using the word in a sentence. Finally, read the sentences together.

Phonics and Decoding Lesson 23

Word Bank

question	invasion	mission
vacation	mansion	station

vaca_ _ _ _   _____

mis_ _ _ _   _____

ques_ _ _ _   _____

inva_ _ _ _   _____

sta_ _ _ _   _____

man_ _ _ _   _____

Dad made a suggestion that
we take a vacation.
We had a discussion.
We took action!

Directions Read each word in the Word Bank. Help your child draw lines between the letters to show the different syllables. Have your child write the letters that make up the last syllable in each incomplete word. Tell him or her to use the Word Bank to check spelling. Then have your child write the complete word on the line. Read the sentences together.

School + Home

feature   picture   nature

pasture   creature   future

capture   vulture   posture

Kelly had a picture of a vulture.
It is a funny creature.

Directions Point to each word and say it aloud. Have your child draw a line before the syllable *-ture* to divide each word into two syllables. Then read one of the words. Have your child point to it and read it. Work together to use the word in a sentence. Continue until your child has read all the words. Then read the sentences at the bottom together.

re + build + ing =

ad + ven + ture =

prin + ci + pal =

lo + ca + tion =

The hippopotamus wandered away from the zoo.
It was terrified by its new surroundings!

School + Home

Directions Model reading aloud the parts, or chunks, of each word on the left. Have your child repeat them with you. Help your child write the parts in the box to form each word. Read the word together several times. Then read the sentences with your child.

shorter   **blackest**   **sickest**

harder   **louder**   **softest**

faster   **coolest**   **quicker**

smaller   **longer**

Sam is faster than my cat.
But the quickest cat is the biggest one.

Directions Ask your child to read each word aloud. Have your child draw a circle around each word that has the ending -er. Then have your child draw a box around each word that has the ending -est. Take turns using each word in a sentence. Finally, ask your child to read aloud the sentences at the bottom.

Base Word	Add -ed	Add -ing
beg	begged	begging
snap		
jog		
rub		
skip		
dip		

The pigs begged and begged.
Quit that huffing and puffing!

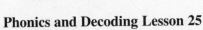
School + Home

Directions Read aloud the first base word, *beg*. Then read aloud *begged* and *begging* and point out how the final consonant was doubled to form new words. Help your child form new words with the other base words. Finally, have your child read the sentences to you.

Name _____

Base Word	Add -*ed*	Add -*ing*
trade		
fade		
dine		
hike		
joke		
poke		
use		

Mom and I hiked to the lake.
We liked wading in the water.

Directions Have your child read aloud the first base word, *trade*. Then model crossing out the silent *e* in *trade* and writing *traded* in the middle column. Write *trading* in the last column. Read the word parts one after the other to read each word aloud. Then help your child continue that process with the other base words. Finally, have your child read the sentences to you.

School +Home

Phonics and Decoding Lesson 25

books	**wigs**	**pencils**
rocks	**tables**	**mugs**
pigs	**socks**	**days**
dolls	**brothers**	**pans**

Pigs in wigs have fun.
The pigs are pals.

Directions Have your child read each word and point to the word part -s. Help your child cut apart the word cards and place them face down. Have your child choose a word. Say a number from two to ten and ask your child to make up a sentence using the word and the number—for example, *I see six red socks*. Repeat with the other words. Finally, have your child read the sentences.

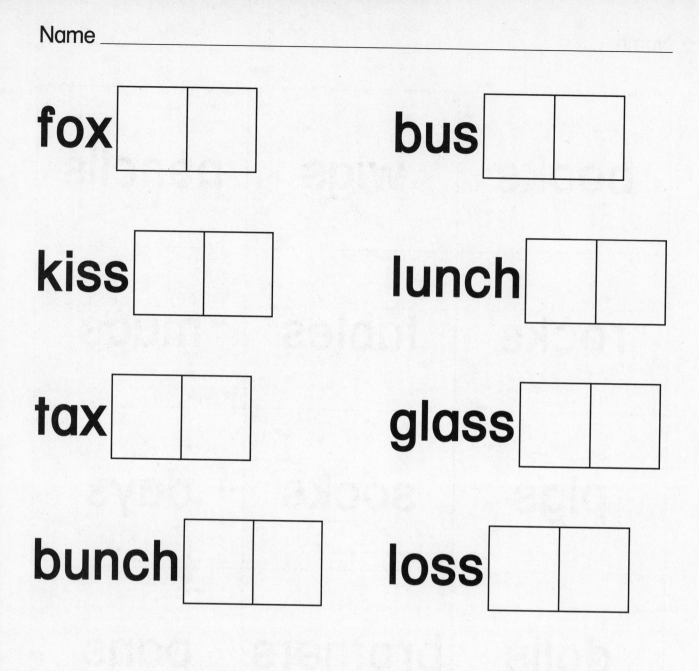

fox

bus

kiss

lunch

tax

glass

bunch

loss

The boxes are small.
Rob tosses the boxes.

Directions Have your child read each word aloud. Ask your child to write -*es* in the boxes to build the plural form of each singular word. Say the new words together. Take turns using each plural word in a sentence. Finally, ask your child to read the sentences at the bottom aloud.

wives	lives	knives
leaves	shelves	loaves

1. leaf _____

2. knife _____

3. life _____

4. loaf _____

5. wife _____

6. shelf _____

The wives used knives to cut the loaves.
They stored the bread halves on shelves.

Directions Point to and read each word at the top. Then help your child cut apart the word cards. Have your child select a card and read it. Help your child place the word next to its singular form. Read both words aloud together. Then have your child write the plural word on the line provided. Finally, read the sentences aloud and point out the six plural words that end in the letters *ves*.

School + Home

Name _____

cake	corn	box
time	pen	hill

1. cup _____ - - - - - - - - - - - - - - - -

2. bed _____ - - - - - - - - - - - - - - - -

3. pig _____ - - - - - - - - - - - - - - - -

4. pop _____ - - - - - - - - - - - - - - - -

5. up _____ - - - - - - - - - - - - - - - -

6. sand _____ - - - - - - - - - - - - - - - -

We played baseball in the backyard.
We did our homework after sunset.

Directions Have your child read each word at the top of the page. Help him or her cut apart the word cards. Read each numbered word and have your child find a word card that can be used to make a compound word. Place the word card on the first line. Then have your child write the compound word on the second line. Finally, have your child read the sentences to you.

School + Home

Phonics and Decoding Lesson 27

Name _____

| sun | snow | way | light |

1.

_____
_____ burn

_____
_____ shine

_____
_____ rise

2.

walk _____
_____

drive _____
_____

hall _____
_____

3.

_____
_____ flake

_____
_____ fall

_____
_____ ball

4.

_____
sun _____

stop _____
_____

_____
flash _____

Ned sees seashells at the seashore.
He spots jellyfish and a starfish.

Directions Read the four words at the top of the page with your child. Help him or her cut apart the two sets of cards. Choose a numbered card and read the words aloud. Help your child find a card with a word that can go with all the words to make compound words. Then have your child write the new word on each line. Read each new word and the sentences aloud with your child.

<u>grass</u>	<u>sun</u>	<u>step</u>
<u>fire</u>	<u>thunder</u>	<u>day</u>
dreaming	fighter	hopper
glasses	storm	ladder

The fisherman wore sunglasses.
It was summertime.
He caught a catfish by the waterfall.

Directions Help your child cut apart the word cards and read each word. Keep the six underlined words and give the other cards to your child. Choose a card, put it down, and read it. Help your child find a word on one of his or her cards that can be added after your word to make a compound word. Have your child put down the word card and read the new word. Read the sentences with your child.

1. sky   _____

2. try   _____

3. reply   _____

4. story   _____

5. fly   _____

Dan saw some dark skies.
Did he bring in the puppies?

Directions Help your child cut apart the cards at the top. Tell your child he or she will use these cards to make new words from the words on the page. Have your child read the first word aloud. Ask your child to cover the letter *y* with the *i* card. Then ask your child to place the *es* card at the end of the word. Have your child write the new word on the line. Repeat with each word. Finally, read each new word and the sentences with your child.

study	tried	reply
copied	replied	studied
worried	try	worry
copy	fry	fried

The baby tried to eat her bib.
Was Dad worried?
No, he just washed and dried the bib.

Directions Have your child read each word, first with you and then alone. Then help your child cut apart the word cards. Ask your child to sort the cards into two piles: words that end in *y* and the same words with their *-ed* ending. Then take turns using each word in a sentence. Finally, ask your child to read the sentences about the baby to you.

School + Home

women	**child**	**geese**
mouse	**men**	**feet**
foot	**children**	**mice**
man	**goose**	**woman**

Six geese chased some children.
Then some men and women used
their feet to scare the birds away.

Directions Help your child cut apart the word cards. Place them face down on a table.
Then take turns selecting a card, saying its word, and turning over another card. If the
two cards show the singular and plural form of the same word, remove them from the
game. If they do not match, turn them over and continue playing. When your child has
matched all the cards, ask him or her to read the sentences.

School + Home

hadn't	I'm	haven't
won't	don't	isn't

do not _____

I am _____

is not _____

will not _____

had not _____

have not _____

I'm eating dinner with Lee.
Isn't corn good?
We won't eat beans.

Directions Help your child cut out the cards and read each word. Have your child read you the list of word pairs on the left. For each word pair, have your child find a contraction that says the same thing in a shorter way. Place the contraction next to the word. Ask your child to write the contraction on the lines. Finally, have your child read the sentences to you.

School + Home

Phonics and Decoding Lesson 29

Name _____

He's	I'd	She's
We'd	He'd	They'd

1. <u>He would</u> like to go.

2. <u>He is</u> not going to play.

3. <u>They would</u> like to eat more.

4. <u>She has</u> moved away.

5. <u>I had</u> met Mike last week.

6. <u>We would</u> like that green car.

She's going to the store.
We'd like to go with her.

Directions Help your child cut apart the cards. Then take turns reading each sentence. Ask your child to choose a card with the word that means the same as the two underlined words in each sentence. Have your child place the card over the underlined words and reread the sentence. Then have your child point to each contraction as you read the sentences at the bottom aloud.

School + Home

Phonics and Decoding Lesson 29

Contractions **87**

You'll	<u>You have</u> fixed some fish.
We're	<u>They have</u> made baked beans.
They'll	<u>We are</u> having a picnic.
I've	<u>I have</u> roasted hot dogs.
You've	<u>You will</u> have fun.
They've	<u>They will</u> bring the drinks.

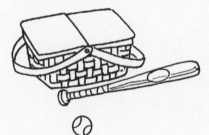

We're glad you're here.
You'll have a great time.
We've planned a fun day.

Directions Help your child cut apart all the cards. Have your child hold the contraction cards, and you hold the sentence cards. Select one sentence card, put it down, and read it aloud. Tell your child to find the contraction that means the same as the underlined words in the sentence. Have your child cover the underlined words with the contraction card. Read the new sentences and the ones at the bottom together.

Phonics and Decoding Lesson 29

puppy	clock's	bike's
family's	kite's	class's
kite	class	family
bike	clock	puppy's

My father's name is Larry.
His brother's name is Barry.
His sister's name is Mary.

Directions Take turns pointing to and reading each word. Then help your child cut apart the word cards. Ask your child to sort the words into two piles: words that are possessives and words that are not. One at a time, choose a word and have your child find the possessive word that matches it. Read both words with your child. Finally, ask your child to read the sentences at the bottom.

Phonics and Decoding Lesson 30

Possessives and Abbreviations **89**

Apr.	1. <u>Doctor</u> James is our new vet.
Fri.	2. She moved here on <u>December</u> 18.
Mr.	3. Her Main <u>Street</u> office is nice.
St.	4. On <u>Friday</u> it's open late.
Dr.	5. <u>Mister</u> Arp thinks she's great.
Dec.	6. She treated his dog on <u>April</u> 1.

On Mon., Jan. 7, Mr. Smith moved away.
Now he lives on Sunset Ave. in Center City.

School + Home

Directions Help your child cut apart the cards. Read each sentence aloud and ask your child to find the abbreviation that stands for the underlined word. Have your child place the abbreviation over the underlined word. Read each sentence again. Finally, have your child read the sentences at the bottom to you, using a full word for each abbreviation.